Matt B[...]

S[...]

Adam Lucas

REDEMPTION

REDEMPTION

Carolina Basketball's 2016–2017 Journey from Heartbreak to History

ADAM LUCAS, STEVE KIRSCHNER & MATT BOWERS

With a Foreword by Roy Williams

JEFFREY A. CAMARATI, *Photo Editor*   J. D. LYON JR., *Principal Photographer*

THE UNIVERSITY OF NORTH CAROLINA PRESS   CHAPEL HILL

© 2017 Tobacco Road Media, Inc.

All rights reserved

Designed by Kimberly Bryant and set in Miller

Manufactured in the United States of America

The University of North Carolina Press has been a member
of the Green Press Initiative since 2003.

Front jacket: photo by J. D. Lyon Jr. Back jacket: photo of
Roy Williams and seniors with championship trophy by
Jeffrey A. Camarati.

Pages ii–iii: photo by Bob Donnan/USA Today Sports Images.

Complete cataloging information can be obtained online at the
Library of Congress catalog website.

ISBN 978-1-4696-3211-7 (cloth: alk. paper)
ISBN 978-1-4696-3212-4 (ebook)

CONTENTS

Hands down, it was the worst postgame meal of my coaching career. It was roughly 90 minutes after Villanova's Kris Jenkins, of all people the adopted brother of our junior point guard Nate Britt, had beaten us with a three-pointer as time expired to win the 2016 NCAA championship. My team had brushed off the confetti meant for someone else, listened to Michael Jordan share how proud he was of them, and gathered in our meeting room back at Houston's Hilton Post Oak hotel.

Our typical postgame spread of grilled chicken, burgers, and fajitas was laid out before us, but I couldn't eat a thing and, for the first time I ever remembered, neither could the players. I'd had the most inadequate feeling of my career in the locker room—there was nothing I could say to take away the heartache of coming so close to reaching our dreams and having it end so cruelly and quickly. I was still searching for something to say to help them. Some of our parents and several of my friends and family came in and tried to console us, but they were thinking the same thing we were: it's so hard to get to the Final Four; will we ever get back and have another chance to be the last team standing to win a national championship?

That awful dinner is where the story of the 2017 national champions be-gins, because I know how hard our players and coaches worked over the next 12 months to rid themselves of the pain they felt after that game. I heard the stories of the players' late-night shooting sessions, saw some really good things in the four practices with our new freshmen in the summer, and no-ticed how focused they were in August and September.

That's why I told them on the first day of practice in October they were good enough to not only play again on the last Monday night but, this time, win the whole blessed thing. Our single-minded goal was to be the last team standing. We were hurt badly last year and didn't want to have that feeling again.

Winning the 2017 NCAA title wasn't redemption for me because Marcus Paige, Brice Johnson, and Joel James weren't there. But our players were all in to try and redeem themselves, get back to the final game, and win the national championship that eluded them a year ago.

It was plainly evident how much they cared. It's why I appreciated their toughness—whether it was Joel Berry dealing with sprained ankles through-out the NCAA Tournament, reminding me of the great Arnold Palmer ac-tually willing the ball into the hole; Justin Jackson fighting through a few games when his shot didn't go in but making plays on both ends of the court to become an all-around All-American; Isaiah Hicks handling some strug-gles, yet making one of the biggest shots a player has ever made for one of my teams; Theo Pinson overcoming injuries twice and being the team's heart and soul, not to mention our best playmaker; or Kennedy Meeks taking the

FOREWORD

Roy Williams and guards Kenny Williams (left) and Nate Britt celebrated as the clock expired in the title game. (Photo by Jeffrey A. Camarati)

Roy Williams and his grandsons,
Court and Aiden. (Photo by J. D. Lyon Jr.)

tough love and playing in several key games at a higher level than any low-post player ever has in my 29 years as a head coach.

I love guys who make sacrifices. Everybody on this team made sacrifices. They all had parents, girlfriends, and relatives saying I wasn't letting them score enough, but the players didn't care as long as our *team* won. They were tough enough to be all in, and that enabled them to play at a really high level in tough situations.

One of the neatest things was how our players reacted after we had pretty much clinched the victory over Gonzaga in the championship game. It was stunning. They had invested so much sweat, attention to detail, and love for each other that you could see the enormity of winning the championship just one year after losing in the last second. It was overwhelming to them.

Kennedy came over to hug me, and I yelled at him to finish the game. There were seven seconds to play, and we had four guys on the court in tears. I've never seen that. I even sent the official over to ask Joel if he needed to calm down before he shot the last free throws because he had tears in his eyes. The players' emotions came pouring out in front of the whole world, and none of them cared because they were all in, all year, and they will carry those memories for all time.

For me, winning this championship was extra special because my grandsons were there to see it. For 24 days four years ago, I thought I had cancer and didn't know if Court and Aiden would know what I did or even who I was. Having them out there on the stage with me was really important and the neatest thing I've ever experienced. Watching those little boys making snow angels in the confetti was cool.

I've been asked about winning three national championships and the company of head coaches that puts me in. I appreciate those numbers, but I don't allow myself to think in those terms because I want to make sure I am just as hungry now as I was in 1989 when I started. I don't want to feel like I've accomplished anything yet. I don't ever want to feel satisfied.

In 2005, we were Led by Our Dreams. In 2009, we enjoyed One Fantastic Ride. In 2017, our players sought and earned their own sense of Redemption. What path will our next championship journey take? Hey, isn't that the fun of getting there?

Roy Williams

REDEMPTION

Justin Jackson remembers that the Golden State Warriors were harsh when he interviewed with them after making himself eligible for the NBA Draft in the spring of 2016.

Following Carolina's loss to Villanova in the national championship game, Jackson entered his name for professional consideration on April 23. NCAA rules allowed him to attend NBA workouts and interviews, plus the NBA Draft Combine in Chicago from May 11 to May 15. Jackson knew he had some areas to improve upon, but he still wanted to hear feedback from professional teams. Golden State gave it to him bluntly.

With the Warriors still in the playoffs, head coach Steve Kerr did not attend the session. But general manager Bob Myers was present, as was Warriors adviser Jerry West—a former Los Angeles Lakers great who is colloquially known as "The Logo" because he inspired the current NBA logo.

"Most interviews are interactive," Jackson said. "The team asks questions and you talk a little bit. With Golden State, I don't think I said a single word that whole 30 minutes. They talked about how I needed to get stronger and needed to shoot the ball better.

"One thing that sticks in my head is their GM [Myers] saying, 'If you think you're working hard now, you're not anywhere close.' . . . Jerry West was kind of blunt, and their GM lit into me a little bit."

It was exactly the kind of feedback the NCAA rule was designed to allow. Jackson had the ability to play in the pros. He would have found a team willing to draft him and pay him a handsome salary to play basketball. But that half hour with Golden State showed him it would be better for him—and, ultimately, better for the NBA team that drafted him—to go back to college with a little dose of reality.

"It hurt my ego a little bit at first," he said. "But it also made me realize that those days when I was tired and said, 'I'll just shoot tomorrow,' that there was so much more that I could do. . . . It helped me realize, 'OK, this might be a job one day.' That was huge for me, and I think hearing it from those guys definitely helped a lot."

On May 16, the day after the combine ended, Jackson told Roy Williams he was returning to school.

Jackson had been joined in the NBA eligibility pool by teammate Kennedy Meeks, a rising Carolina senior who had submitted his name in tandem with Jackson. His professional aspirations were part of a busy spring for Meeks, who had also pledged the fraternity Kappa Alpha Psi. The decision to join a fraternity—a time-consuming process—was an unusual one for a Tar Heel basketball player and required some explanation to Williams. But Meeks had some family ties to Greek life on campus in Chapel Hill, and he had been interested in pledging since his freshman year.

1

RESHAPING THE ROSTER

Confetti fell after Villanova beat UNC in the 2016 NCAA championship game. (Photo by J. D. Lyon Jr.)

Once he began the NBA process, Meeks received an even ruder reception than Jackson, but it didn't come in the form of harsh criticism from NBA executives. Instead, Meeks wasn't even one of the approximately six dozen players who received an invitation to the Combine in Chicago.

"I thought for sure I would be invited," Meeks said. "That hurt me. It was heartbreaking."

Their different but equally stern NBA responses sent Jackson and Meeks back to school and solidified the 2016–17 Tar Heel roster. Without either one of those players, the Tar Heels would have had a significant hole in their rotation. With both, though, they were suddenly one of the most experienced teams in the Atlantic Coast Conference, despite the loss of three important scholarship seniors—Brice Johnson, Marcus Paige, and Joel James—who had played key roles in the drive to the 2016 national title game.

Williams was in good spirits when he took his annual golf trip to Phoenix with his wife, Wanda, and a group of their close friends. As usual, he brought the season highlight video, which ended with Paige's remarkable three-pointer that tied Villanova in the championship game.

Most outsiders believed Carolina's national championship window had closed with the departure of Paige and Johnson, both of whom earned the right to have their jerseys honored in the Smith Center rafters. But Williams knew his team had a chance to be nationally competitive again, depending on the progress made in the off-season by a few key players. Jackson's acceptance of Golden State's unforgiving message was the first step. The head coach knew enough about the Jackson family to suspect that Justin wouldn't pout about another year in college. But even Williams wasn't prepared for the rigorous summer upon which Jackson embarked.

■ When Luke Maye arrived on campus in the summer of 2015, he quickly found a willing workout partner in Carolina head basketball manager Chase Bengel. Every weekday, Maye would text Bengel: "What are you doing tonight? Let's get some shots up."

Maye's idea of a workout wasn't a simple 30-minute shootaround, though. It wasn't unusual for a session to stretch to two hours, with Maye firing jumper after jumper and Bengel rebounding every shot. Eventually, Bengel had to mandate that the pair take at least one day off per week.

During the course of his freshman season, Maye had found a connection with Justin Jackson. Both Tar Heels shared a strong family background and a deep religious faith. Jackson, who had been homeschooled, spent his freshman year a little wide-eyed at details as seemingly mundane as the huge crowds at the Smith Center.

Ironically, Jackson had played in the Smith Center plenty of times before signing his letter of intent to Carolina, just not in front of a crowd. He first

Tar Heels past and present gathered at the 2016 Roy Williams Carolina Basketball Summer Camp. (Photo by Jeffrey A. Camarati)

attended basketball camp at Carolina the summer after his fifth-grade year and also returned as an older player, playing in camp games in the Smith Center.

College basketball camps are different from college football camps, which are often designed to identify top prospects. It's much more unusual for a staff to find a top recruit at a basketball camp. But when Jackson came to Chapel Hill for camp as a middle schooler, Roy Williams noticed him.

Williams was making his usual rounds of that day's camp action. The head coach makes it a point to watch games in every gym during his camp because he wants every participant to feel that they have received the ultimate Carolina Basketball experience.

While walking through Carmichael Auditorium—there's only enough room for the oldest players to play at the Smith Center during camp—Williams spotted a player with potential.

"He was on the far court, away from the old basketball office," the head coach remembered. "I saw this skinny kid make a nice pass, and I said, 'Nice pass.' I walked to the middle court and then walked back. And he did it again. I said, 'That's two really nice passes.' Then he made a nice little move and took it to the basket. As I was leaving Carmichael, Steve Robinson was going

in. I told him, 'Check out the little skinny kid on the other end of the court. I think you will know who I am talking about.'"

The little skinny kid, of course, was Justin Jackson, who went on to become one of the most sought-after recruits in the country. But when he arrived at Carolina before his freshman year, he had never played in front of a true home crowd before. His high school team had been made up of fellow homeschooled students and traveled to other gyms to find opponents. Now, as a Tar Heel, Jackson had nearly 22,000 people screaming for him at every home game and thousands against him on the road.

During practice, it wasn't unusual for Jackson to knock down a dozen three-pointers in a row. Everyone who watched him shoot outside of games marveled at his smooth stroke and unlimited range, but in games, he wasn't finding a rhythm. He shot just 30 percent from the three-point line as a freshman and saw that mark dip to 29 percent as a sophomore.

Jackson came from a basketball background and benefited from parents who were very in tune with his game. His mother, Sharon, played at Blinn Junior College; in the fall of 2015, she told Jackson he was getting too much lift on his jumper. He corrected it and promptly went out and won MVP honors at the CBE Hall of Fame Classic in Kansas City.

Whether struggling or succeeding, Jackson maintained the same demeanor. Teammates marveled at the very rare times he was motivated to bark at an opponent on the court. He was regularly one of the most engaging Tar Heels when the team participated in community activities, and it wasn't unusual to find him lifting up a Special Olympian for a dunk at the team's annual clinic. He had a serious girlfriend, a basketball player at Florida, but the couple seemed connected more by their interest in charity work than by their ability on the basketball court.

Outsiders sometimes wrongly interpreted Jackson's even keel as a lack of passion for the game. He was relentlessly humble, but he also admitted the tough words from the Warriors had stung him. In the summer of 2016, now motivated to use the constructive criticism he'd received from NBA teams, he found another thing in common with Luke Maye: a love for the gym.

"I'm going to shoot with Chase," Jackson told Maye one day after class.

"Do you mind if I come?" Maye asked.

From that point on, the two were close to inseparable. Their daily routine was simple: a 7:00 A.M. weightlifting session with Carolina strength and conditioning coordinator Jonas Sahratian. Class. Lunch, followed by a shooting session. Homework, dinner, and another shooting workout, which was often followed by a third late-night trip to the Smith Center to take even more shots.

"Every time I'd come to the gym, I would hear the ball bouncing in the practice gym," said Joel Berry II. "I'd go put in my code to check and see who

Every time you walked in the gym, you saw Justin doing something to better himself. From that point on, I knew he was going to have a great season.

—JOEL BERRY II

All-America Justin Jackson and Hall of Fame Coach Roy Williams confer during the South Regional final. (Photo by J. D. Lyon Jr.)

was there, and it was Justin. The next time I'd come to the gym, he would be there again. Every time you walked in the gym, you saw Justin doing something to better himself. From that point on, I knew he was going to have a great season."

One of the most helpful parts of the NBA education process for Jackson had been the on-court workouts, which often contained new drills or unique shooting exercises. He brought some of those elements back to Chapel Hill and implemented them into his off-season work. The routine in the gym wasn't the same every day, but it always focused on shots that Jackson and Maye might shoot in a game. It wasn't just spot-up three-pointers. It was a mixture of one-dribble pull-up jumpers, coming off a screen, or sprinting to the corner. Every day wasn't perfect, but the partnership meant that when Jackson was frustrated, Maye would build him back up. And when Maye's jumper wasn't falling, Jackson was there to remind him of the progress they'd made.

"When he decided he wasn't going to the draft, we got together and said we had to improve our shooting," Maye said. "I had to improve so I could be on the floor, and Justin said the big thing the NBA teams told him is he had to shoot it better from three. We worked on it every day. . . . We didn't really compete against each other, but I definitely knew how many he made and how many he missed. We both love competition, so being able to go back and forth with him all summer showed me how to work and how to compete."

Roy Williams told his team on the first day of practice that they were good enough to win a national championship. (Photo by Jeffrey A. Camarati)

Maye and Jackson, almost always joined by Bengel, became constant workout partners. Maye's fellow rising sophomore, Kenny Williams, often joined them. Weekday or weekend, it didn't matter—there were always shots to be taken, even while the rest of campus was busy hitting Franklin Street and enjoying the warm Chapel Hill summer nights.

As with every Tar Heel, part of the Jackson/Maye workout plan included daily pickup games at the Smith Center with the current team and the host of alums who return to Chapel Hill in the summer. The games are well known, which is a draw for other high-level players. A myriad of unlikely players have participated over the years; for example, NC State's Ilian Evtimov—the brother of former Tar Heel Vasco—was a regular attendee during his Wolfpack career. Even Gerald Henderson, a Duke alum despised in Chapel Hill for his vicious elbow that broke Tyler Hansbrough's nose in 2007, came to play pickup during his Blue Devil tenure.

But none of those players was as unlikely as the appearance of Villanova forward Kris Jenkins in Chapel Hill during the summer of 2016. Jenkins' relationship with rising Carolina senior Nate Britt was well documented. Britt's parents became Jenkins' legal guardians in 2007, and the pair played together on multiple teams as kids.

Only their college basketball allegiances separated them. When Carolina and Villanova played each other in the NCAA Tournament in 2013, Britt and Jenkins—both committed to their school of choice by then—watched the game from separate ends of the same room, not talking to each other. Their post–national championship conversations in 2016 had been typical of brothers, focused less on Jenkins' epic shot and more on the handful of possessions when Britt had guarded Jenkins.

Because of the different academic calendars at their respective schools, Jenkins had always been able to visit Chapel Hill during Carolina's summer school, where he would play pickup. But that was before he broke Tar Heel hearts with his championship-clinching shot in Houston. "We can go in the gym and work out," Britt told Jenkins when they were discussing their summer Chapel Hill plans. "But I don't know if the guys are going to want to play pickup with you."

Britt consulted with Marcus Paige to find out if the departing senior would mind sharing the court with Jenkins. Paige told Britt he should ask his teammates to confirm no one had a problem with it. Britt also had a close relationship with former Tar Heel point guard Kendall Marshall, whom he grew up idolizing in the Washington, D.C., area. Because of Marshall's early departure for the NBA, the pair were never UNC teammates, but they worked out together regularly. Marshall echoed Paige's sentiments, so Britt sent a message to the team's group chat asking for thoughts on playing pickup with Jenkins.

Carolina began its title chase on October 3rd, 183 days before beating Gonzaga for the national championship. (Photo by Jeffrey A. Camarati)

The response was unanimous, and perhaps best expressed by Theo Pinson: "Bring him down here so we can go at him," wrote Pinson, as usual mixing his competitiveness with his typical brand of good humor.

As everyone expected, Jenkins played without incident. The games were actually much less tension-filled than those that included Henderson, who played in pickup games against the legendarily competitive and highly motivated Hansbrough.

It was a revealing window into the culture of modern college basketball. Both Henderson and Jenkins were outsiders with a long history with at least one Tar Heel (Henderson was a longtime friend of Wayne Ellington). But Henderson had made what some viewed as a dirty play; Jenkins' only transgression was making a classic shot every Tar Heel dreamed of making. While the sight of Jenkins on Franklin Street did prompt some occasional catcalls from Carolina students whose hearts were still mending, he took very little grief from players inside the Smith Center. Yes, he made the shot that devastated the 2016 Tar Heels. But it wasn't personal, it was basketball. Every player on that team knew how close the game had been, and if the championship game was ever mentioned, several Tar Heels were quick to point out that if it had gone into overtime, Carolina had all the momentum.

(L) UNC celebrated the start to the season with its annual mix of skits, dances, and ball at Late Night with Roy. (Photo by J. D. Lyon Jr.)

(R) Assistant coach Steve Robinson goes the selfie route with freshmen Shea Rush and Tony Bradley. (Photo by Brian Batista)

Ultimately, the reason every Tar Heel was hard at work in the gym that summer was to try and earn the opportunity to make a championship-winning basket in 2017. As the players developed—Jackson was blossoming, players and alums who faced freshman Tony Bradley in pickup games were buzzing about him, and Joel Berry II was coming off a transformational finish to his sophomore year—their optimism about the upcoming season grew. The Villanova game stopped feeling like an ending, like the closing of a window, and started to feel like the natural step on the progression to a championship.

The players renamed their group chat "Redemption." When told in July that the new name felt a little optimistic, Meeks responded, "It's something we want to go back and do. We have an opportunity to do it. What better response could we have than to go back and win it?"

As usual, Williams spent early July on the high school recruiting circuit. His recruiting drive is virtually unmatched, even among his peers. It's not unusual for the Tar Heel head coach to scan the schedule of that day's high school games and say, "Well, this game isn't going to be any good, but let's go watch it anyway." There is a misperception that Williams enjoys golf as much as basketball. The reality is that the links are a distant second to anything related to his team. Ask Williams' closest friends if he would rather play golf or run a Tar Heel practice, and the answers are quick and unanimous: he'd much prefer to be in the practice gym.

Williams spent a full July day at the Peach Jam in Augusta, Georgia, and was due at another recruiting event in Spartanburg, S.C., the next day. He made the two-hour drive with longtime friend Cody Plott. As usual, the talk turned to basketball. Williams was frank about his team's prospects for 2017. "We have to get a whole lot better at a whole lot of things," he told his friend. "But I really think we have the chance to be pretty good."

With the exception of a handful of practices, NCAA rules prohibit Williams from overseeing his team's day-to-day summer workouts. But over the next month and a half, word circulated throughout the Smith Center about the renewed dedication from the players, led by Jackson, who Williams felt was one of the keys for 2017. "The number of extra shots Justin got up during the summer," the head coach said, "was phenomenal."

So while much of the rest of the basketball world was lamenting the loss of Paige and Johnson, Williams was quietly confident about his upcoming team. On the first day of classes in August, he put the Tar Heels through their normal yearly conditioning test. Then they met as a group at Williams' home.

His preseason message isn't always the same. He wants to set the bar high enough to force his team to reach to achieve it, but he also wants to give them a realistic goal. If Jackson had turned pro or Berry didn't have leadership potential or there were known chemistry issues, perhaps Williams would have composed a different message. But even with a difficult schedule and the prospect of perhaps the best conference depth in Atlantic Coast Conference history, the Hall of Fame head coach knew exactly what he wanted to say to his team.

"In this room," he told them, "is a team good enough to win the national championship."

Luke Maye was all business at Late Night, the traditional start to Carolina's basketball season. (Photo by J. D. Lyon Jr.)

The Tar Heels had been so close to a national title in 2016 that it's only natural the topic came up more than normal during the preseason. Or perhaps the number of mentions wasn't necessarily higher, but the gravity of each was increased.

Roy Williams broached the subject with his team again during a September conditioning session at the Smith Center. The afternoon's workout had already included grueling circuit training, followed by two sets of 16 sprints from sideline to sideline in a minute or less, capped by four 33's (a 33 is three trips baseline to baseline and back in 33 seconds or less).

It was perhaps the toughest day of conditioning of the preseason, and a couple players didn't make their required times. That meant more running until they met the requirements. When those players stepped to the line, they found that they were joined by several teammates—including Luke Maye and Justin Jackson, plus seniors Nate Britt, Kanler Coker, and Stilman White.

At the conclusion of practice, Jonas Sahratian led the team in stretching, and then Williams addressed them. Tiny details had been accentuated during the sprints—touch every line, make every turn the right way, finish all the way through the line. There was a reason for the emphasis.

"You guys who weren't here last year, ask the guys who played in that game," Williams told his team. "If they had it to do over again, they would play harder. At the time, they thought they were going as hard as they could, but when they look back, they wish they could do a little more. It's the little things."

Veterans silently knew exactly what Williams meant. Kennedy Meeks had shot one-for-eight in the championship game, and some of the misses were makeable shots. Justin Jackson had missed a layup through contact at the end of the first half that would have stretched the Carolina lead to nine; the Wildcats made a jumper on the other end as time expired to cut the deficit to just five. The four-point turnaround, in what was ultimately a three-point game, had troubled Jackson all summer.

Senior Isaiah Hicks had grabbed just four rebounds in 20 minutes and battled foul trouble, collecting four personal fouls. Always a homebody, Hicks regularly had made the 45-minute drive from the Smith Center to his hometown of Oxford during his first three summers as a Tar Heel. Before his senior year, however, he committed to staying in Chapel Hill. Even during the break between summer school and the fall semester, he spent time in the gym.

"I knew if I went home, it wouldn't be as intense working out there as it would be working out in Chapel Hill with Jonas [Sahratian], especially in the weight room," Hicks said. "I wanted to maintain what I had done all summer until the school year started."

His commitment showed, and Hicks was in very good shape for the start

2
ADVANCED CHEMISTRY

Freshman Brandon Robinson and sophomore Kenny Williams got the season off to a flying start at Late Night with Roy. (Photo by J. D. Lyon Jr.)

of conditioning. That type of focus and sacrifice was what had the head coach excited about his 2017 team. Outside the Smith Center, basketball observers were emphasizing the loss of two key players from last year, and Carolina was generally outside the national top five in most polls. But inside the Smith Center, Williams had lofty goals for his team.

"We were that close to winning a national championship," Williams told them as he held his thumb and forefinger a couple of millimeters apart. "That close. When you get that close, it's those little things that make the difference."

It was one of those cold-chill moments Williams frequently mentions. Almost everyone in the gym knew what it felt like to have come "that close" in Houston. And all the Tar Heel players and coaches were imagining what it would feel like to finish the quest in 2017.

■ The unofficial first road trip of the season took place in October on a quiet trip to Fort Bragg to practice in front of the base's soldiers. By March, road trips would all seem routine. But in October, especially for the newcomers, it was a new experience. Subconsciously, the players left open the seats usually occupied by Brice Johnson and Marcus Paige.

"Wait a minute," Joel Berry II said as the team sorted through the seating arrangement. "Marcus and Brice aren't here."

The comment echoed a stern point made by Roy Williams at a practice earlier that week. When the Tar Heels lackadaisically pursued a rebound, Williams blew his whistle and stopped practice. "Do you see Brice out here?" he asked of the 2016 All-America who grabbed over ten rebounds per game. "He's not here! He's not coming back!"

In one very important way, however, the presence of Johnson and Paige did linger. When that duo had arrived in the summer of 2012, along with classmates Joel James and J. P. Tokoto, the Tar Heel chemistry was different. It wasn't a bad environment, but on a 16-player roster, there were several different groups that rarely mixed. They were close-knit in the locker room, but you would rarely find upperclassmen like Reggie Bullock or Leslie McDonald mixing with rookies like Paige or James.

Paige, who was well-respected from his first day in the program, was treated as a veteran leader by the time he was a junior. Once he was a senior, the tenor of the locker room changed. "We never really made a conscious effort to make sure everyone was hanging out together, but that's what happened," Paige said. "We did everything in big groups. When a couple guys were going to do something, they'd always see if everyone else wanted to go. I don't know if any other team has as much fun as we did. Everyone enjoys college. But the 2016 and 2017 teams, I don't know if there are any other teams since Coach has been back that have had as much fun as we did."

Nate Britt and Theo Pinson at Fort Bragg.
(Photo by J. D. Lyon Jr.)

Seventh Woods, Joel Berry, and Kenny Williams. (Photo by J. D. Lyon Jr.)

Roy Williams took his team to practice at Fort Bragg, the largest military installation in the world. (Photo by J. D. Lyon Jr.)

As coaches, we're not responsible for just teaching kids how to box out and shoot. We're responsible for showing them experiences that help them have an even broader perspective.

—ROY WILLIAMS

If a player went and saw a new movie with a date on the day it was released, it wasn't unusual for that player to go back with the entire team days later to see the same movie, just to be part of the group.

The realities of college basketball travel, especially at a program like Carolina, mean the team often arrives back in Chapel Hill via charter airplane in the middle of the night after a road game. After the bus ride back to the Smith Center, numerous players often would travel in a pack to a local grill that stayed open until the wee hours of the morning. The team also discovered a Chapel Hill pizza joint that featured $2 pan pizzas after 10:00 P.M.; it became a regular haunt after late-night workout sessions.

"Even when we get a break from each other, we still end up doing stuff together," said Nate Britt.

Friendships never put points on a scoreboard, of course. But the players are convinced the chemistry of the past two years made a difference. It's not typical to be able to throw together strangers from Apopka, Florida; Oxford, North Carolina; and Tomball, Texas, and have everyone get along. Chemistry is not guaranteed and can sometimes be elusive. This group had it.

"You've got guys from so many different backgrounds," Paige said. "But we always went out as a group or went to the gym as a group. Every day in practice was fun, but we were also pushing each other. And then you'd find that after practice guys were sitting in the locker room for hours talking about who got the best of whom and how it won't happen tomorrow. That all goes back to Coach Williams and the type of people he wants to bring into the program. It sounds like a humble brag, but it made a difference with our teams that even though everyone had different life experiences, there was a common background that you knew you were dealing with quality guys."

"It was kind of like Marcus and Brice's class looked out for us," Britt said. "And now it's our time to look out for the next class."

Even with Paige and Johnson chasing their professional basketball dreams—and therefore having vacated their coveted seats in the back of the team bus—it was a lively trip to Fort Bragg. The trip was something Williams had tried to arrange for several years, but the timing had never been conducive.

In October, with the able coordination of director of operations Brad Frederick, the Tar Heels were able to pull together an afternoon journey to Fayetteville, where the military base hosted a UNC practice that was open to all Bragg personnel. The new location created a different environment. During prepractice stretching, for instance, a fan walked onto the court to high-five Kennedy Meeks, then wrapped Williams in a bear hug. "These are my boys!" the fan shouted, and practice continued.

The team handed out Tar Heel Basketball t-shirts and gear after the practice, then adjourned to 1BCT DFAC, better known as the Devil's Den dining area. Players and coaches spread throughout the dining hall to sit and talk with soldiers, who were a little surprised to find a college basketball team in the chow line. The similarities between the two groups were jarring. Both the Tar Heel players and the soldiers were largely 18-to-22-year-olds. But the 18-to-22-year-olds living at Fort Bragg talked matter-of-factly about multiple deployments to the Middle East. Assistant coach Steve Robinson chatted with Will Romer, who had only been in the military for approximately a year and was younger than Justin Jackson, but who already had 14 parachute jumps, with a 15th planned for the following evening. It was a stark reminder that there were bigger issues in the world than free throws or offensive rebounding.

"Our soldiers in the 82nd are constantly training for deployment and are very busy, so they rarely get the opportunity to conduct community engagements," said Captain Lisa Beum, who is stationed on the base. "But this one was definitely special. They felt appreciated, and it gave them the chance to show what they do day-to-day, whether it's cooking for thousands of soldiers in the dining facility or conducting training. . . . The interaction was a wonderful opportunity to see the differences, but more importantly, the similarities between soldiers and civilians."

The highlight of the evening came after dinner—the head of the dining hall had been quick to point out that he was a Duke fan, but the food still seemed edible—when two Polaris MRZR-4 vehicles pulled up outside. Players quickly lined up for a ride around the base in what were basically souped-up, four-seater dune buggies.

Of course, as they strapped on their combat helmets for what promised to be a high-speed dash through muddy and water-filled areas, they still had their priorities. Players had just received brand-new, team-issued Jordan brand sneakers. One by one, they carefully removed the shoes and piled them on the sidewalk, not wanting to risk a mud splotch on the new kicks.

After the team boarded the bus and departed the 251-square-mile base, Roy Williams sat in his normal front right seat and reflected on the day's activities.

"Our world is fantastic, but it has a few problems," the coach said. "We are very lucky to have men and women like the ones we met today who do some great things and make sacrifices to allow the rest of us to do what we do. As coaches, we're not responsible for just teaching kids how to box out and shoot. We're responsible for showing them experiences that help them have an even broader perspective. That's what today was about."

Williams' teaching background often showed up on Tar Heel road trips. The day at Fort Bragg was planned exclusively to show his team another side of real life. But even on normal basketball trips, he often tried to find a way to include an educational activity.

President Barack Obama met with the basketball team for the third time when he visited campus in November. (Photo by Jeffrey A. Camarati)

Carolina journeyed to Memphis in late October for the NCAA-allowed closed preseason scrimmage. The mood was a little somber because Theo Pinson had suffered a fractured foot at practice the week before, his second such injury during his Tar Heel career. Teammates had been virtually unanimous in declaring him the most likely player to have a breakout season; now the timeline for his season debut was uncertain. But Pinson was buoyed by the fact that the injury was not season ending. He hoped to be ready for conference play and still accompanied his teammates to Memphis.

The day before the scrimmage, Williams took his team to the National Civil Rights Museum at the Lorraine Motel, the site of the 1968 assassination of Dr. Martin Luther King Jr. Every year Williams has taken a team to Memphis as a head coach, he's made a stop at the museum.

This time, though, he had an additional experience planned for his team. One of the head coach's closest friends is Rusty Carter, a North Carolina businessman who often accompanies the team on road trips. Carter was with the Tar Heels in Memphis, and he was standing in the hallway outside the UNC locker room later that afternoon after practice.

Suddenly, assistant coach C. B. McGrath peered out of the locker room. "Rusty," McGrath said. "Coach wants you."

Since the days of Dean Smith, the Carolina basketball locker room has been sacrosanct. Very few outsiders are permitted, and even fewer address the team.

Isaiah Hicks scored 16 points as Carolina defeated UNC Pembroke, 124–63, in a preseason exhibition game. (Photo by Jeffrey A. Camarati)

But the explosive nature of race relations in America means the Civil Rights Museum can be a grim visit. Williams wanted his team to understand not just the conflict in their nation but also some lesser-known pieces of history.

"The museum can be very harsh," Williams said. "It's white on one side and black on the other. I thought it was important for them to know it's not always like that, and there were white people who thought what was going on in our country was wrong."

Carter's father, Horace, was a Carolina graduate who ran the *Tabor City Tribune*, a weekly newspaper he had founded in 1946. Through his editorials in the paper, he spoke out against the Ku Klux Klan in the small North Carolina town, an unpopular position that resulted in threats against both the newspaper and Carter's family. The *Tribune* won a Pulitzer Prize in 1953 for Carter's work, and his story has been chronicled in books and documentaries.

Rusty Carter is also a Carolina graduate and grew up with a deep understanding of his father's contributions to the state. Getting the opportunity to stand in front of the UNC basketball team—Horace Carter was a loyal Tar Heel hoops fan who would have been thrilled at the notion of his son addressing the team—and talk about his father was very emotional for him. "My dad would have loved that moment," Carter said. "It brought together so much of his own journey, plus the enlightenment and legacy at Carolina, and to see today's African American players who followed Charlie Scott all com-

Juniors Justin Jackson, Joel Berry, and Theo Pinson vowed as freshmen to win a national championship. (Photo by Jeffrey A. Camarati)

ing together under Coach Williams' influence was very special. That's exactly why my dad risked it all in his passion for racial justice."

With the room completely silent, Carter told the players about his father's struggle for what he believed was right, and about how proud he would be of the character of everyone in the room. Every eye was on Carter, and the room was completely silent. No one checked a phone. No one shuffled his feet.

"Carolina is a place that changes lives," Carter told the team with tears in his eyes. "My father would tell you it absolutely changed his life and enabled him to have an impact on lots of people. It changed my life. And it will change your life, if you'll take advantage of the opportunity you are being given, not just to play basketball there but to attend school there."

"You could have heard a pin drop," Williams said of the rapt attention given to Carter by the players.

Kenny Williams started 22 of the first 26 games before a season-ending knee injury. (Photo by Jeffrey A. Camarati)

"To see the things that I saw throughout that museum made me appreciate how it is today," said Berry. "I always ask myself, 'How would I respond if I was back in the day in that moment?' There were some strong people who went through it and were able to fight through it. To hear Mr. Carter talk about his dad, it was obvious he really cared about it and cared about what he does and what his dad did. That changed my whole perspective on life. Regardless of anything, you have to treat people with respect. That's what I got from that trip."

During his coaching career, Williams has taken his team to Memphis approximately a half dozen times, but, given the political climate in America in the fall of 2016, that visit might have been the most powerful of any of them.

"It was a very eye-opening experience," said Justin Jackson. "We were there at the same time there was some stuff in the news about police brutality, and some of the guys on the team were angry and upset about that. To hear Mr. Carter talk about his dad and the things he did for the African American race, I think that was very helpful to my teammates in showing them that not everyone is out there to do you wrong."

Off the court, Williams very rarely tells his team what to believe. But he does make an effort to show them multiple sides of an issue and to remind them they are in a very fortunate situation. Six months later, very few players recalled details of the scrimmage against Memphis. All of them, however, remembered the locker-room lesson.

The education continued on Carolina's early-season trip to Hawai'i. Before Thanksgiving was over, the Carolina Basketball program would already have racked up approximately 11,000 air miles.

The regular season had begun with a road win at Tulane. The trip to New Orleans was memorable mostly for an interaction on the bus ride to shoot-around that emphasized the youth of the Tar Heel players. As the bus passed the New Orleans Superdome, the site of Carolina's 1982 and 1993 national championship victories, Roy Williams turned around to face his team.

"Does anyone know what two famous games happened there?" he asked.

The bus was silent. Finally, Joel Berry II ventured a guess: "Wasn't that where Alabama won the BCS title?"

The head coach grinned. They were exceptionally talented basketball players, but sometimes they were just kids. Williams explained the significance of the building, and then the Tar Heels opened the drive for another national title with a win nearby in the season opener later that evening.

The team then returned home and collected home wins against Chattanooga and Long Beach State. With one of Roy Williams' favorite November tournaments, the Maui Invitational, on the schedule, Carolina had also scheduled a game at the University of Hawai'i before heading to Maui.

The Long Beach State game ended late on Tuesday night and the game at Hawai'i was tipping off at 1:00 A.M. Eastern time late Friday night, so the Tar Heels departed for Hawai'i on Wednesday. The over 13-hour series of flights arrived in Honolulu around 4:00 A.M. Eastern time, meaning the players arrived at the hotel about the time their bodies told them it was almost time to wake up—only to discover it was actually time to go to bed in Hawai'i.

It's not exactly an extreme hardship to play basketball in Hawai'i, but it was obvious the Tar Heels' biorhythms were affected by their travel schedule. They mostly lumbered through a 15-point win over the Rainbow Warriors.

It's a well-established rule of Carolina Basketball road travel that the head coach is ready to depart the arena as soon as possible after a game. Williams does his press conference, the players shower, and the bus is idling outside the locker room door shortly thereafter. Especially after a bad performance, no one wastes time getting on the bus, lest they delay the gentleman in the front right seat.

What happened after the win over Hawai'i, then, was notable. Several players had already gotten on the bus, not wanting to risk being left at the arena. That's when Williams was reminded that the crew of the nuclear submarine USS *North Carolina* had attended the game. That crew, captained by Durham native and Tar Heel fan Gary Montalvo, had invited several members of the program to tour the sub earlier in the day. The crew had adopted

3

BUILDING A FOUNDATION

Joel Berry's goal was to join the list of Tar Heel point guards who had won MVP honors in Maui, a goal he accomplished after scoring 18 points per game in the three wins. (Photo by J. D. Lyon Jr.)

Coach Williams greeted Navy Commander
Gary Montalvo, a Durham native and skipper
of the nuclear submarine USS *North Carolina*.
(Photo by J. D. Lyon Jr.)

the identity of the "Tar Heel Boat" and posted Carolina gear throughout the
sub.

"Let's take a picture with them," Williams said. He'd already taken the
players on a tour of Pearl Harbor, but that was more of a historical trip. This,
like the trip to Fort Bragg, was an opportunity to remind his team that while
playing basketball was important, some of their peers were doing even more
significant work.

"Some of them are already on the bus," the head coach was told.

"I don't care," he replied.

That's how the team came to be lined up on the Stan Sheriff Center court
with dozens of sailors, the Tar Heel Boat crew and the Tar Heels together for
a photo at around 3:00 A.M. on the body clocks of the Carolina players.

■ The moment was quintessential Roy Williams. Not Roy Williams the Hall
of Fame basketball coach, but Roy Williams the high school teacher, the
young man who got his coaching start while teaching physical education at
Owen High School in Black Mountain, North Carolina. Today, over four decades removed from that position, it's sometimes easy to see Williams only as
the famed coach who drives a shiny new car and frequently travels via private
jet. At times, though, little glimpses into his personality reveal he has more
in common with the Owen High coaching staff than with other high-profile
coaches.

The Tar Heels paid respects at the USS *Arizona* Memorial at Pearl Harbor. (Photo by J. D. Lyon Jr.)

That's probably because Williams never really began his coaching career with the goal of being a high-profile coach. At the time he was coaching the Owen Warhorses, most young coaches in the state of North Carolina wanted to be Dean Smith. Williams knew of Smith and had done some work for him as an undergraduate student at Carolina, but a much more realistic goal was for him to be Buddy Baldwin—the longtime high school coach who had mentored Williams and was, as Williams says, "the reason I went to college."

Even today, Williams will quickly tell you that his mother was his hero. Lallage Williams was a hard worker who was completely devoted to Roy and his sister, Frances. Roy Williams idolized her, even though he understood his family did not have money. While other students were getting their driver's licenses as soon as possible, for example, Williams waited until 11th grade because he did not want his mother to feel obligated to buy him a car.

But it was the exposure to Baldwin at Roberson High School in Asheville that opened Williams' mind to coaching. Not coaching at North Carolina—nothing as grand as that. He would have been thrilled with the opportunity to just emulate Baldwin. He eschewed an offer to go to Georgia Tech and study engineering and instead enrolled at Carolina. The first two times he traveled home from Chapel Hill, he hitchhiked.

Early in his Carolina tenure, Williams met another transformative person in his life: Wanda Jones.

"The first part of our freshman year, my girlfriend would come and see

Breaking down the Hawai'i game video in the airport as UNC headed to Maui. (Photo by J. D. Lyon Jr.)

me and stay with Wanda in Cobb Dormitory," Williams said. "And Wanda's boyfriend would come and see her and stay with me in Hinton James. About halfway through the year, we decided to get rid of the middle people."

Wanda was as feisty and capable as Lallage Williams, but with an added bonus: she came from an extremely close-knit family, the type that Roy had always dreamed about. The summer after the couple's freshman year, Williams would have dinner with the Jones family almost every Saturday night. He looked around the table and could not believe his good fortune.

"Until I started dating Wanda, I'd never had a family dinner together," Williams said. "I can't remember my family ever being together like that. I only have one photo of my sister, my mom, and I all together. So Wanda gave me the family I wanted to have but didn't have."

The Saturday evening dinners became a family tradition. As soon as he became the Kansas head coach, Williams politely but firmly told Wanda's parents—who have now been married for 67 years—that he would be paying for all future meals when they dined out together. "I still think I'm ahead," he said, "because of all those Saturday night meals."

Wanda Jones did not marry a future high school coach with the notion that one day he would be in the Basketball Hall of Fame. She married Roy Williams assuming that they would continue to do exactly what they did for his first coaching job at Owen: every morning, they'd make bologna and mayonnaise sandwiches and place them in Ziploc bags for the players on his team because many of the players were too poor to afford snacks before practice.

In Wanda, Williams had found the perfect partner.

"I decided I wanted her to be the mother of my children," Williams said. "I knew she would be the best mom I could ever imagine. I wanted somebody I loved and trusted and somebody I could be with, but for me it was important to have somebody be a great mom, because of the life I had growing up."

They grew into what friends call "the closest couple I know." Wanda's complete trust in her husband helped jumpstart his career. After the couple had their first child, Scott, Dean Smith offered Williams a low-paying assistant coaching job to come back to Chapel Hill. At the time, Wanda was not working but had arranged for a job at Tuscola High in Waynesville to supplement Williams' coaching income.

"Let me get this straight," Wanda said when Roy brought her the job offer. "They're going to pay you $2,700 per year. You're going to make $16,000 this year at Owen, and I'm going to make $14,000 at Tuscola. We've got a new house and a baby boy and you want to go back to Chapel Hill."

Put that way, the decision seemed obvious.

"That's right," Williams said, a little sheepishly.

Wanda had only one response: "When do we leave?"

Down time in the airport in Honolulu was an opportunity for the coaches' and staff's kids to hang with the players. (Photo by J. D. Lyon Jr.)

Now, of course, the choice seems simple—the Williams family would enthusiastically accept the job that would pave their way to more money and fame than they could ever have imagined. But when they were making the choice, the only sure bet was that in Chapel Hill they'd be earning less than a tenth of what they would make in the mountains. The finances were so bleak that both Roy and Wanda inquired about taking on paper routes in Chapel Hill.

Forty years later, their life together—the way they interact, not the trappings of being the Carolina basketball coach—hasn't changed much at all. Roy Williams oversees anything that has to do with sports. He rolls the trash can and recycling to the road once per week. He takes clothes to the dry cleaners. And Wanda Williams does most everything else, including handling the finances. She also reads voraciously, only bringing an article to her husband's attention if she thinks it is noteworthy.

Perhaps she is right to take the lead with the finances. After a strong run

of success at Kansas, Roy Williams received a call from the university chancellor, Robert Hemenway, telling him it was time to restructure his contract to reflect his status as the best college basketball coach in the country.

The chancellor filled in the legal part of the document and left the financial side blank. "Just fill it in," he told Williams. "Fill in the years and fill in the money."

"That was pretty powerful," Williams recalled. He took the paper back to his office and gave it some consideration. He eventually called Hemenway and told him he'd made his decision. With the opportunity to push his contract into the financial stratosphere, he instead wanted the same financial structure he'd always had. But there was a very serious situation that was bothering him. He sometimes had to park on the fifth floor of the parking deck near Allen Field House.

"I would really like that first parking spot on the ground floor," he told Hemenway.

Hemenway paused, waiting for the rest of the demands. "And that's it?" he asked.

"That's it," Williams said.

"I think we can do that," the chancellor replied.

While Williams was out earning those contracts, Wanda was raising two children, Scott and Kimberly, a feat that still makes her husband marvel. Roy did the little things when he could. He made a promise to both kids that they would never see him napping on the couch when they were home. Before the kids left for school on many frostbitten mornings in Lawrence, Kansas, it was their father who cranked their cars to warm the interiors for them. Wanda did all the carpools and the teacher conferences and the after-school activities.

It was perhaps the only way the arrangement could work. Outsiders see Roy Williams' job as being six months a year, the length of a regular season. In reality, it is nonstop. When the games end, the recruiting begins. Easter weekend is one of Williams' favorite holidays of the year. In Philadelphia during the 2016 NCAA Tournament regionals, he even found time to hide eggs for his grandchildren on the morning of the regional final. But when Easter fell later during the 2017 season, after the championship, he carved time out of his holiday weekend to make recruiting calls.

There are perhaps some college coaches capable of separating themselves from their job, or, more importantly, from their program. But there is not a day out of the year that Williams is not thinking about University of North Carolina basketball. If he's not coaching the team on the court, he's talking to a class on campus—he is also frequently asked by coaches of other UNC sports to speak to their recruits—or attending a Rams Club meeting, or writing a letter to a Tar Heel fan who is battling cancer. Every day, whether walk-

Freshman Tony Bradley scored 13 points in UNC's 107–75 win over Oklahoma State. (Photo by Jim Hawkins)

Joel Berry enjoys a light moment with Coach Williams during practice in Lahaina. (Photo by J. D. Lyon Jr.)

Carolina flew a whopping 27,246 air miles during the 2016–17 season, which is believed to be the all-time program record. Some of those trips were lightning-fast, in-and-out journeys that were little more than a stopover. On back-to-back Saturdays in January, for example, the Tar Heels were on the ground in Boston and Miami for less than 24 hours each to play Saturday afternoon ACC road games.

Other trips had an educational component. Through a connection with the director of the Smith Center, Angie Bitting, the Tar Heels enjoyed a tour of Pearl Harbor in Honolulu. Over 1 million people per year visit Pearl Harbor, but the team had their own private remembrance barge for a solo trip to the USS *Arizona* Memorial.

That same trip to Pearl Harbor also exposed the Tar Heels—a techno-savvy group prone to appreciating the latest technology—to the X-band radar housed on the base. The approximately $6 billion radar, which looks like a tiny Epcot ball, requires 400,000 gallons of fuel each time it is refilled and can detect an object as small as a tennis ball anywhere between Pearl Harbor and San Francisco.

While memorable sports settings are often a benefit of Carolina road trips—under Roy Williams' direction, the Tar Heels have played in venues as diverse as the historic Palestra in Philadelphia to the palatial AT&T Stadium in Dallas and have taken a private tour of the Basketball Hall of Fame—there are just as often side trips highlighting wider culture for the players' education.

Williams has taken past teams to the Martin Luther King Jr. Center in Atlanta. During the head coach's tenure in Chapel Hill, the Tar Heels have visited an Air Force base in Arizona and eaten a meal with the midshipmen at the Naval Academy. They've toured the Santa Monica Pier and the New York Stock Exchange. The Tar Heels have made one trip to the White House (several players had never seen the major Washington,

Justin Jackson and Coach Williams depart the USS *Arizona* Memorial in Pearl Harbor. (Photo by J. D. Lyon Jr.)

Carolina fans gave Kanler Coker and his teammates a spirited send-off at the Peabody Hotel in Memphis. (Photo by J. D. Lyon Jr.)

D.C., monuments, so the team bus circled by some of the most important ones).

"I want our trips to be educational and more worldly when we have the opportunity," Williams said. "I don't want to just stay in the hotel and listen to music and lay in bed all day long. I want them to see different sites and different places, and visit places they will read about in history that will be important to them."

And even with the usual pre–road trip stops at local restaurants like Raleigh's Angus Barn and the Chop House, players most often recall the unique team

meals on the road as trip highlights. With so many different destinations, 2017 was a notable dining year for the Tar Heels. On back-to-back weekends during the postseason, the players enjoyed meals at two of the very best restaurants in America at their specialties: Hall's Chophouse for steaks in Greenville, South Carolina, and Rendezvous for ribs in Memphis.

"Rendezvous was really, really good," said Justin Jackson. "It was such a cool experience being able to go in there. It's one of my favorite places we've been since I've been here."

ing down Franklin Street or traveling on vacation or sitting at dinner in a restaurant, he *is* North Carolina basketball.

Always with him, usually in the background, is Wanda. It has only been recently that he relented and allowed her to ride on the team bus; his previous rationale had been that she was not on the team and therefore should not travel on the bus. But after virtually every game, he'll return home and ask Wanda what she thought about it. She admits to not being a basketball guru, but he likes getting the view from the stands and hearing some of the unfiltered commentary. And don't take Wanda's lack of tactical knowledge for a lack of passion: after one memorably listless Carolina performance several years ago, she pointedly told her husband the team had played horribly—then offered to write him a check to cover his fine from the ACC so he could criticize the officiating. (He declined.)

They completely trust each other to perform their designated roles. When the couple decided to build a beach home near Charleston, Roy Williams had a simple question for the builder: "Do you have any problem dealing with women?" The builder laughed, but Williams was serious. He wanted to sit on the porch and enjoy the ocean breeze; Wanda would be in charge of blueprints and design and specs. And that's how the house was built, a refuge the family still enjoys.

Williams' current players mostly know Wanda as a willing host for their occasional team gatherings, including the annual Selection Sunday parties at the Williams home. She's frequently by the coach's side on road trips, and at least one Tar Heel veteran noticed the unique relationship. Kennedy Meeks was the first player in recent memory to inquire with the couple about how their relationship worked.

"Coach is so outgoing and talkative, and Mrs. Wanda is so quiet," Meeks said. "Sometimes you wonder how they met, or how she likes him. I wondered how she dealt with Coach on a daily basis, and I soon realized that she is a very aggressive person. She definitely tells Coach when he needs to do stuff or when he needs to be quiet sometimes, and I feel like he listens to her. He may not say it to us, but I think she sometimes puts him in his place."

Meeks laughed when reminded that at one point during the 2016–17 season, Wanda told her husband to stop being so hard on Isaiah Hicks.

"What she should have told him," he said with a grin, "is to lay off me a little bit."

■ There was no reason for the head coach to chasten Meeks in Maui. The senior big man posted a pair of double-doubles, including a 20-point, 10-rebound performance against Chaminade, followed by a 15-point, 16-rebound showing against Wisconsin in the championship game.

At the Tar Heel practice at the Maui Civic Center the day before the games

Joel Berry, Isaiah Hicks, and Justin Jackson prepared to go snorkeling in the Pacific Ocean. (Photo by J. D. Lyon Jr.)

(Photo by J. D. Lyon Jr.)

Thanksgiving Day afforded Isaiah Hicks and his
teammates time to enjoy Maui's ocean adventures.
(Photo by J. D. Lyon Jr.)

began, Berry was stretching while he looked at the arena's banners. One
listed the tournament champion and MVP for each season of the event.

In 2004, North Carolina won the Maui Invitational and Raymond Felton
claimed MVP honors. In 2008, the Tar Heels again won the tournament,
with Ty Lawson earning MVP accolades.

"At that point, I told myself, 'You know what, I'm going to put my name
up there with those guys, because those are the guys I looked up to before
I came here,'" Berry said. "I meditated on that the whole time we were in
Maui. I thought about me playing as well as I could and my team holding
up the trophy at the end. It was a huge honor for me to win the MVP, but to
see our team come together with the younger guys and the older guys, you
could start to see it happening for our team. It was great to be able to live in
that moment."

The team's Maui title was the highlight of a trip that was another boost for
team chemistry. Williams is fond of saying he doesn't recruit anyone whom
he wouldn't trust to babysit his grandchildren. The Maui trip was packed
with young members of the traveling party, with at least a dozen children on
the over-one-week trip.

There were times it was difficult to separate the kids from the players.
In the airport on one leg of the journey, while Isaiah Hicks played his ever-

Coach Williams' pregame tradition—
a search for and a wave to Wanda. (Photo by
J. D. Lyon Jr.)

present video games, a group of kids enlisted Theo Pinson and Joel Berry for their game at the airport gate. Other players sat and watched, cheering when the kids scored on the Tar Heels.

Roy Williams sat at an adjacent gate with his staff, watching film of Carolina's next opponent on a laptop. Nearby was Wanda, enjoying some time with the couple's daughter, Kimberly, who was on the trip. Occasionally, one of Berry's young playmates would wack him on the head with the ball. His teammates roared; Wanda looked on from afar and grinned.

Virtually every Tar Heel basketball practice starts the same way. In pairs, players split up among eight baskets stationed around the Smith Center court. There, they spend several minutes doing that most basic of basketball drills: working on shooting form. The focus is on the form, not the result.

Early in the season, Justin Jackson and Joel Berry II were paired at a basket. Jackson had been playing extremely well, and even during shooting-form drills, the rim looked enormous. "It feels like high school out here again," he said to Berry.

"I had so much more comfort and confidence this year," Jackson said. "Freshman year, it was like a chicken running around with his head cut off. Then you start settling in, and sophomore year gets better. This year, it was a totally different feeling. It felt good just to be playing again."

After seven straight wins to start the season, including the Maui title, the Tar Heels faltered for the first time at Indiana. It was a classic case of catching a team at the wrong time: the Hoosiers brought in the members of their 1981 national title team for a reunion, Chicago Cubs World Series champion and IU alum Kyle Schwarber was on hand, and fans lined up outside the newly renovated Assembly Hall in the early afternoon for a 9:15 P.M. tipoff. The nine-point loss was less indicative of Carolina's shortcomings than it was of the reality that in college basketball, any talented team can summon one heroic evening, especially at home.

The Tar Heels picked up three more wins after the visit to Bloomington, with two of them coming without Berry, who was nursing an injured ankle. That gave Nate Britt the chance to play an important role late in the two-point win over Tennessee, which was sealed by a key blocked shot from Tony Bradley.

But even the last-second win over the Volunteers was mostly just a prelude to the most anticipated game on the nonconference schedule: a date with Kentucky in Las Vegas. The Wildcats and the Tar Heels are two of the most consistently excellent programs in college basketball. A semiregular home-and-home series was annually one of the signature games of the first two months of college hoops, but this year the matchup moved to a neutral site as part of the CBS Sports Classic.

Typically, Carolina travels on the day before a road game. The team attends class in Chapel Hill, practices at the Smith Center, eats dinner together, and then departs for the airport. It's not unusual, if the game is early in the afternoon on a weekend, for the Tar Heels to be in the destination city fewer than 24 hours. The Vegas trip would be the rare road trip for which Carolina was scheduled to leave two nights before the game. With a Saturday tip and a long, time-zone-crossing trip to Las Vegas, Williams opted to leave one day earlier than normal.

4

WHAT HAPPENED IN VEGAS

Luke Maye scored in double figures for the first time as a Tar Heel in the win over Davidson. (Photo by Robert Crawford)

Seventh Woods had six points in UNC's largest comeback win of the season against Tennessee. (Photo by Peyton Williams)

Kenny Williams scored a career-high 19 points against Radford. (Photo by Jeffrey A. Camarati)

At least, he tried to leave one day earlier. When the team assembled at RDU International Airport for the charter flight to Las Vegas, they found no aircraft awaiting them. The plane eventually arrived, but bad weather had detained the scheduled pilots in another city. Facing the prospect of not leaving until midnight or later, Williams sent everyone home and asked them to reconvene early the next morning. The bus took the team back to the Smith Center. With a late arrival back to the arena and an early departure the next day, most of the staff spent the night in the newly renovated locker room and players lounge.

Even once the team landed in Las Vegas, it still didn't feel like a typical road trip. The Tar Heels held one practice at T-Mobile Arena. With CBS broadcasting the game, longtime analyst Bill Raftery was on hand. Raftery, one of the friendliest people in college basketball, was a close friend of Dean Smith and is well connected to the Tar Heel program. He was joined at practice by former Tar Heel player Doug Moe, who spent 15 years as a head coach in the NBA and is one of the biggest characters in the Carolina family.

As the Tar Heels went through drills, Moe and Raftery told stories and entertained each other. The conversation got a little rowdy, which is unusual for a Carolina practice, which are usually businesslike affairs. Just like Dean Smith, Williams schedules his practices down to the minute. If a drill is listed as ending at 1:36, it ends at 1:36. The head coach believes players being able to trust the practice plan builds their trust in the coaching staff.

Two basketball lifers guffawing on the sideline are not usually part of the practice plan. As he left the court, Williams was asked if the rowdy conversation bothered him. "Nah," he said. "That's just Moe."

■ Game day turned out to be about as freewheeling as that conversation at practice had been. The Las Vegas Strip location, plus the always-huge Kentucky traveling contingent, gave the game a circus atmosphere. Elvis impersonators mixed with Minnie Mouse and other costumed characters on the concourse, and the halftime show featured a showgirl on roller skates. The basketball game itself was every bit as electric.

Recently, Kentucky and Carolina have built successful programs through different approaches. The Wildcats are a hotbed of one-and-done talent, coached effectively by John Calipari and then pushed to succeed at the pro level, making room for the next crop of outstanding youngsters. Nine Wildcats had been chosen in the NBA Draft in the previous two seasons, and five players from the 2017 team would declare early.

Williams has taken another path, and not necessarily by choice. He had recruited several of the Kentucky players, for example. But the Wildcats were the current favorite of the turn-pro-quickly crowd, and the Tar Heels were also dealing with some frustratingly inaccurate innuendo on the recruiting trail.

Instead, Williams was in a successful cycle of identifying talented players who also won't give up, even when faced with challenges that might have been unfamiliar given their basketball backgrounds. Brice Johnson is a primary example. For the previous four years, Williams had coaxed and cajoled Johnson to improve. The South Carolina native was a solid player but not a superstar—until his senior season in 2016, when he exploded into All-America status and had one of the most productive seasons of any Williams big man.

Kennedy Meeks was in the process of following the same blueprint. He'd entered as an overweight freshman and had steadily lost weight each year of his career, watching his production increase correspondingly.

Williams and his coaching staff deserved credit for sticking with their plan, for emphasizing the same details every day in practice even when it felt

Nate Britt scored 11 points and tied his career highs with seven assists and five steals against Tennessee. (Photo by Peyton Williams)

Joel Berry scored 23 points and had seven assists in the loss to Kentucky in Las Vegas. (Photo by J. D. Lyon Jr.)

like they weren't being heard. But the players also ignored the sometimes quick-rewards nature of college basketball and persevered even when they were frustrated. Williams found the delicate balance of identifying players who not only wanted to improve personally but also were driven to get better because they were committed to making their team better.

On the 2017 team, it was Jackson who best embodied this modern Carolina approach. Although he'd sometimes been overwhelmed as a freshman, Jackson had been a highly rated recruit and had a unique combination of size and skill.

Johnson had gone from never making an All-America team to a first-team All-America pick in 2016; one year later, Jackson would make the same leap forward. His return to school for his junior season eventually netted him approximately $10 million more over four years than he would have made if he had stayed in the NBA Draft following his sophomore campaign.

Jackson was terrific in Carolina's 103–100 loss to the super-talented Wild-

Carolina avenged its loss to Northern Iowa from a year earlier with an 85–42 win four days before Christmas. (Photo by Jim Hawkins)

cats in Las Vegas. He scored 34 points on a variety of offensive moves that included his signature midrange shots and four three-pointers.

Despite the divergent backgrounds of their programs, Calipari and Williams don't coach all that differently on the court. Both preach up-tempo basketball but also try to sell their players on the importance of defense.

Calipari gets more attention for running NBA sets, but in the 2017 NBA playoffs, the San Antonio Spurs often ran one of Carolina's favorite plays: a box-left elevator set the Tar Heels ran frequently to get Jackson an open three-pointer at the top of the key. Jackson was unusually aggressive in the Kentucky game, taking 15 free throws—more than he had attempted in the previous five games combined. Against one of the most talented teams in college basketball, Jackson didn't seem out of place on the court. His 36 minutes played were more than anyone else on the team. If his Maui performance hadn't already done it, his Kentucky showing was the one that thrust him into early-season consideration for national honors. Here was yet another Tar Heel who had struggled, learned, and was now blossoming into one of the country's best players.

The Las Vegas setting and the high-profile matchup meant scouts from virtually every NBA team were on hand to watch Carolina and Kentucky. Jackson had a mature outlook on the next step of his basketball career.

"I think today people are way too consumed about the NBA and trying to get there as fast as possible," he said. "I talked to Coach after my freshman and my sophomore years about trying to get to the NBA. Everyone I talked to about it always told me, 'It's not how fast you get there. It's how long you last there.' Some of the guys that are one and done will be in the league for a long time. But I felt like I had so many things I needed to get better at so that once I got to that point, I could stay there.

"I think that's the same with Brice, and I think that's the same with a bunch of people who have come through this program. I get sick and tired of people saying that Coach tries to hold people back or that he wants to keep people here longer than they should be. In reality, if someone came in here and averaged 18 or 19 points per game, Coach would say, 'It's your time to go.' You have to be able to succeed at the college level first. What I think Brice and I have shown is that maturity is important, and it's something guys trying to get to the NBA should not overlook."

Williams is known for putting in extensive time on the recruiting trail, getting to know a prospect. Some coaches do most of their recruiting on the AAU circuit; Williams also likes to watch a player extensively with his high school team if possible.

He's looking for a fit with his basketball team, of course; every recruiting season means holes that need to be filled and a roster that needs to be reshaped. But he's also seeking players and families who want to be part of the

I talked to Coach after my freshman and sophomore years about trying to get to the NBA. But I felt like I had so many things I needed to get better at so that once I got to that point, I could stay there.

—JUSTIN JACKSON

At the same time the Tar Heels were playing some of their most intense games of the season, they were also participating in some of Roy Williams' favorite off-court activities.

Every fall, Williams organizes team basketball signings. Everyone on the squad signs hundreds of basketballs, which are then sold to UNC fans around the country, some of whom FedEx their order forms overnight priority just to ensure they receive one of the coveted pieces of memorabilia.

The proceeds from those sales then fund another of Carolina's traditions: a holiday shopping trip for underprivileged families. The money is already in place, so Williams—who hosts an annual breakfast on the first day of the season that has raised over $1 million to fight cancer—could easily send the office staff to do the shopping. But he wants the players to participate, so players are given a shopping list by an area charity and walk the aisles of a local store to select the items that are the best fit.

Every player has a spending limit, and girlfriends and coaches' wives are often a major help in making the right choices. As usual, the players can't subvert their competitive instincts for very long; by the time they've completed their selections, they're comparing purchases with teammates to determine who came closest to the spending limit without exceeding it.

Theo Pinson and his teammates enthusiastically embraced the shopping trip for needy families, a holiday tradition at Carolina. (Photo by Matt Bowers)

A month later, Williams' staff organizes the annual Special Olympics clinic, which brings Special Olympians from dozens of counties across North Carolina to the floor of the Smith Center. It's a tradition Williams began while head coach at the University of Kansas. Often, the Tar Heel players seem to get as much out of the day as the Special Olympians do. For some, it's the first time they've been exposed to that type of active community service. It doesn't take long, though, before they're laughing and helping their charges slam home a dunk on the lowered Smith Center goals.

Dean Smith helped establish Carolina as a program with a broad world view. Although Smith didn't often invite the public inside the program, he made constant efforts to expose his players to life beyond basketball. Under his direction, the Tar Heels made multiple unpublicized trips to visit prisoners. As a player under Smith, Eric Montross became involved with the North Carolina Children's Hospital. That connection has now spanned generations of Tar Heels, as it was Montross who first invited Luke Maye to visit the Children's Hospital with him. Maye now makes regular unannounced visits to the facility; he ate lunch with a nine-year-old patient the day after his game-winner against Kentucky.

"While we're players here, it's bigger than us," said Joel Berry. "We get all the attention and everybody focuses on us, but when we get to do things like the Special Olympics clinic, it's awesome to be able to see the smiles on their faces.

"It's the best feeling for me that I can play basketball and still have an impact on somebody else. That makes me want to continue to be a better person, because wherever you go, no matter what you're doing, there is always someone who is looking up to you, and you're always motivating someone in their life to be a better person as well."

Theo Pinson (pointing, center) sat out the first
16 games due to a broken bone in his right foot.
(Photo by J. D. Lyon Jr.)

way he runs a program. He's going to push them hard, and he needs players
who will respond.

"He's going to try to get the best out of you," said Theo Pinson. "At eigh-
teen and up, you're hard-headed. You know you know it all, but he knows
what he's talking about. When we do what he says, and we win, you're just
like, 'Wow, he was right.' It comes down to how much he cares about his
players. He cares about everybody equally. He treats Joel Berry just like he
treats Kanler Coker. He takes care of everybody as much as he can, and tries
to get everybody in the position where they can do something after they leave
Chapel Hill. There's a reason everybody comes back here. It's because of that
man [Williams]."

■ Of course, Williams is also fiercely competitive. And so it infuriated him
that his team played so poorly defensively against Kentucky. The defeat was
the first time in his tenure at Carolina that his team had lost while scoring
at least 100 points in regulation. Kentucky freshman Malik Monk's 47 points
were the second-most ever scored by a Tar Heel opponent.

Given the atmosphere in Bloomington, the loss at Indiana had felt almost unavoidable. The Kentucky game, though, featured multiple opportunities to steal a win. And so, while Williams didn't mention it in his postgame press conference, Pinson's absence might have played a role. It's not that he could have locked down Monk; as Pinson himself observed from the bench, "I don't know if anyone can stop him right now." But it would have given the Tar Heels one more body to throw into the defensive rotation.

The usually bubbly Pinson was solemn after the game. In a departure from the normal team travel plan of sprinting to the airport after a road game, the team had a few hours before leaving for the charter flight home. Pinson went out to eat on the Las Vegas Strip with Berry and Berry's sister, where the group talked about what a great game it had been. The trio agreed Pinson would have made a difference.

"It felt terrible to know you could help out your team, but you can't do anything about it," said Pinson. "It was tough to just watch. It was a tough one for me. But right after the game, I told everybody we were going to see them again. I just knew we would play them again."

The only possible rematch would have to come in the NCAA Tournament, as both teams were just a couple of weeks from entering conference play. Carolina was still in the national top ten, but the pair of recent losses had dimmed some of the optimism of the Maui title.

Among outsiders, that is. Players and coaches tend to have a little broader perspective on what can be a very long season. Berry was frustrated with some of the missed opportunities against Kentucky. But he was also realistic about what it meant for his team.

"The Kentucky game was the best game I had ever been involved in to that point," Berry said. "I love being a part of a game like that, with a fast pace and great players on the court. It showed us we could play with high-level teams. Theo didn't even play, and we were right there with them. I just knew if we saw them again and had Theo, we were going to beat them."

Tony Bradley scored eight of UNC's 100 points vs. Kentucky in Las Vegas. It was the first time UNC lost a game in regulation when hitting the century mark. (Photo by J. D. Lyon Jr.)

Carolina held a three-point lead at halftime over Georgia Tech in the Atlantic Coast Conference opener for both teams on December 31. And in the Tar Heel locker room during the intermission, well . . .

"I went wacko," said Roy Williams.

Just as the loss to Kentucky had contained some encouraging aspects, sometimes a lead comes with disappointing factors. That was the case in Atlanta, where a Yellow Jacket team picked as one of the worst in the league was somehow hanging with what seemed to be a disinterested Tar Heel squad.

Even months later, as he talked about what turned into a 75–63 loss to Tech, Williams was still fuming about the game.

"It was a twelve o'clock game, we were fat and happy," Williams said. "At that point in the year, nobody thought Georgia Tech was going to be any good. We weren't playing hard, and we weren't into it mentally. We thought we were going to win just by going out there."

The head coach wasn't as concerned with the result. He knew the conference was tough and knew his team would lose a game or two before March. It was the way his club played that concerned him. He gave them a pointed message before the team boarded the bus.

"You have a choice," he said. "You can play like this, and it will be a season that's over quickly. Or you can change, and we have a chance to do great things. But we will not do great things playing like this. Don't tell me this means something to you and then come out and play like that. That was a 100 percent breakdown of your mental preparation to play the game."

The head coach called it "one of the lowest levels to which I've ever had a team play." The loss was on a Saturday, and Carolina's next game was at Clemson on Tuesday. That gave the coaching staff approximately 48 hours before the plane would leave for Clemson to turn their team's mindset around. Williams, as usual after a loss, slept very little the next couple of nights.

What fans sometimes miss when they only see Williams exhorting his team on the sideline during a game or shouting pointed instructions to a player during a timeout is that coaching is much more than what happens during the two hours on television once or twice a week. Away from games, Williams has grown into a coach who takes a much longer perspective on a season.

"It still destroys me when we lose a game," he said. "But I've gotten much better at understanding that at the end of the year, that loss won't make much of a difference. In 2012, we lost to Florida State by 33 points and still won the ACC regular season and went to the regional final. My focus is more on getting them better and better as the season goes on, not on beating someone up because we lost one game. As I've gotten older, I've done a better job of understanding how long the season is. What makes the difference is how you play at the end."

5

DISASTER
AVERTED

Kenny Williams scored six points in overtime at Clemson in UNC's first ACC win of the season. (Photo by Robert Crawford)

Hip-hop recording star J. Cole visited the Tar Heel locker room after UNC's 107–56 win over NC State. (Photo by J. D. Lyon Jr.)

Justin Jackson showed off his questionable dance skills in the UNC locker room after beating NC State. (Photo by J. D. Lyon Jr.)

And so, after heatedly making his point in the Atlanta locker room, Williams altered his message at practice before the trip to Clemson. Now, it was less about what his team had done wrong against Georgia Tech and more about where they wanted to go with their season.

Returning players from the 2016 team had already been talking openly about their desire to return to the Final Four and challenge for a national championship again. Now, at 0–1 in the ACC, Williams put the challenge back on them.

"Everybody tells me you want to get back to the Final Four," he told his team. "But you're not doing the work to show me you want to get back. Tell me again: what was the most fun you've ever had in basketball?"

The room was unanimous: making the run to the 2016 national championship game.

"Then let's pay the price," Williams said. "If you want to get back there, we can't practice like this. We can't play like we did at Georgia Tech. You tell me last year is the most fun you've ever had. Well, that's what should drive you. It's not that we lost. It's that we want to go back and have that same amount of fun again. But let's keep in mind one thing: we don't just want to be there on Monday night. We want to be the last team standing. But you have to be willing to practice and play the way that will help us get back there."

Kennedy Meeks had 18 points, 11 boards, three blocks, and three steals at Wake Forest. (Photo by Robert Crawford)

■ The loss in Atlanta, as Williams said, "shook" his team. They responded to his message with seven Atlantic Coast Conference victories in a row, including a gutsy overtime win at Clemson, road wins at Wake Forest and Boston College, and an important home victory in a raucous Smith Center over ninth-ranked Florida State.

The seventh straight win, however, came with a price. With eight minutes left in the first half of a 91–72 victory over Virginia Tech in Chapel Hill, Theo Pinson left with an apparent foot or ankle injury. He eventually returned to the bench in street clothes with two minutes left in the game, but his injury cast a pall over what normally would've been a boisterous postgame locker room. Instead, players sat silent. Unfortunately, Pinson had extensive experience with foot injuries. He knew how this one felt—and it wasn't good.

"It was an emotional locker room," Williams said. "It was one of the tougher scenarios I have ever walked into. He had worked so hard to get back, and he was doing some nice things. It was a crusher emotionally when he went down the second time, because we all had the fear he would be out for the year. That was one of the toughest couple of days I have had, because I was so afraid he was done."

The win over the Hokies was on a Thursday; Carolina was due to play at Miami on Saturday. As the possible courses of treatment became apparent, team athletics trainer Doug Halverson went to Pinson's apartment, where he was accompanied by director of player development Eric Hoots and director of player personnel Sean May. They found a despondent Pinson, the TV off, his head in his hands.

"I was just sitting there crying," Pinson said. He had maintained an extremely positive outlook during his comeback from the foot injury suffered in the preseason. He'd remained engaged with the team and had taken to sitting in the vacant seat of assistant coach Steve Robinson on the team's trip to Hawai'i, when Robinson had to stay home due to a blood clot. He enjoyed being "Coach Pinson," offering little tidbits of advice to his teammates.

But he enjoyed playing more. And the initial prognosis after Thursday night's injury was not positive.

Pinson's father was already in Miami, where he had traveled to watch Saturday's game. Halverson, Hoots, and May consoled Pinson. "I'm scared to tell my parents," he told them.

Pinson's parents are some of the most gregarious and well-liked of all the Tar Heel parents. It seemed unusual to be scared of them.

"I know how much they were looking forward to this season," Pinson said. "It's going to be really tough for them. It's going to hurt my dad a lot."

The trio from the staff assured Pinson his parents could handle the news. They called Theo Sr. and told him some of their concerns about his son's foot.

Freshman Brandon Robinson scored six points, his ACC best, against NC State. (Photo by Jim Hawkins)

Isaiah Hicks had 22 points in UNC's win over No. 9 Florida State. (Photo by Jeffrey A. Camarati)

Justin Jackson matched his career high with 10 field goals en route to 26 points in UNC's 19-point win over the Hokies. (Photo by J. D. Lyon Jr.)

"Dad, I'm so sorry I let you down," the younger Pinson said. "I didn't want this to happen. I don't know what we're going to do."

Both Pinsons were in tears, as were Halverson, Hoots, and May. That's when the elder Pinson provided the perspective only a parent could share.

"Theo, don't you ever think I'm not proud of you," he said. "Don't ever think that in your entire life. You've represented our family the best you possibly can for your whole life. I am nothing but proud of you, all the time."

The moment went from being devastating to uplifting. Later in the day, Pinson went back to the Smith Center, where he met with Roy Williams. "Coach, I need to be on the court," he told the head coach. "We have a chance to win the national championship."

"We do have that chance," Williams agreed.

"If I'm out there, I can help," Pinson said. "I can do some of those little things you need us to do to help us win games. I'm going to do whatever it takes to be able to help. And I don't think this is the same injury. I've hurt my foot before. I know what it feels like. This is not the same thing. I don't think it's the same injury."

"We're going to try and get some more information," Williams told him. Downstairs, the coaches told the rest of the team about Pinson's uncertain

Luke Maye grabbed a career-high 15 rebounds against an athletic Florida State team. (Photo by Jeffrey A. Camarati)

Theo Pinson announced his return to the lineup with a thunderous dunk against the Seminoles. (Photo by Robert Crawford)

Isaiah Hicks scored 20 in the 85–68 win over Syracuse, Roy Williams' 800th as a head coach. (Photo by Robert Crawford)

Carolina went 8–0 at the Smith Center in ACC play, including a 91–72 win over Virginia Tech.

(Photo by Peyton Williams)

Nike presented
Coach Williams with
a special pair of Air
Jordans after he won
his 800th game as a
head coach.
(Photo by Peyton
Williams)

Carolina survived a mild scare with an 80–78 home win over Pitt. (Photo by Jeffrey A. Camarati)

situation. Pinson stayed in the basketball office, and the coaches suggested to Joel Berry II, his longtime roommate, that he should stop by and see his friend.

The two have been close since before they arrived at Carolina. But this was the first time that Berry wasn't completely certain what to say to his roommate.

"I just stood outside the office for a little bit," Berry said. "I was trying to find something to say because, at that moment, there's really nothing you can say. Nothing you can say changes the fact that his foot is hurt.

"When I went in, I tried to keep it as simple as possible. I let him know that the team and me personally were completely behind him, and we would get through it."

Team doctors told Pinson he could not play against Miami while they pursued other opinions. Initially, he did not want to accompany the Tar Heels to Coral Gables. But coaches and players persuaded him he was needed, as much for the team's mental state as for his own. Pinson's leadership and fun-loving personality made him an essential part of the team chemistry. No one else was willing to joke with Williams the way Pinson did. No one else knew just when to fire a zinger—while never making it mean-spirited—at a teammate to take him down an appropriate number of notches.

Pinson's on-court personality—pass first, set up teammates, figure out a way to help the team—carried over into the locker room.

"He's always thinking of somebody else," Jackson said. "When you have someone who is a starter but who has the mindset of, 'All I care about is my team,' that makes everybody come together more. Inside the locker room, when things aren't going as great as you need them to go, to have someone like him who is always encouraging people is huge for a team's success."

The team, in many ways, took on Pinson's personality. And as much as he wanted to try and be positive in Miami, it was frustrating to once again be wearing a suit while his teammates competed against an ACC opponent. It was hard to tell if Pinson's mood was fueling Carolina's struggles, or Caro-

A water crisis in Chapel Hill delayed UNC's home game against Notre Dame for a day and forced its move to the Greensboro Coliseum. (Photo by Jeffrey A. Camarati)

Isaiah Hicks had 10 points and UNC held
Virginia to 41 in its home win over the Cavaliers.
(Photo by Jeffrey A. Camarati)

lina's struggles were causing Pinson's mood. At one point, the Tar Heels went through a 1-for-19 shooting stretch. Around that same time, Isaiah Hicks sat on the bench with his arm around a clearly distraught Pinson.

"He kept saying, 'Why did I have to get hurt?'" Hicks said. "I told him he can't worry about that. He just has to worry about getting better."

Miami won the game, 77–62, snapping Carolina's winning streak. Berry lost his composure and picked up a technical foul, Kennedy Meeks got a little chippy on the bench, and the offensive execution was subpar. Players and coaches realized the outcome of the game had fewer ramifications than Pinson's health moving forward. But they also knew they had let the concern about their teammate affect their effort, something they had pledged would not be a problem after the loss at Georgia Tech.

This might normally have been a moment when Pinson would have spoken to the team. Instead, the reprimand came from a somewhat unlikely source: the usually reserved Justin Jackson. The junior addressed his team in the locker room with a loud—especially by Jackson's standards—message.

"There were some things I didn't like as far as how guys were acting," Jackson said. "So I told them, 'We have to put everything aside individually. We can't play like we just played and get back to the Final Four. It doesn't matter if I hurt your feelings or not. We are all trying to get back to that last Monday night and win it.'

"At the time, I think everybody was kind of upset with me," Jackson said. "But when people sat back and thought about how we had played in that game, they knew that was not what we needed to do the rest of the season."

They also knew they needed a healthy Pinson. After initial dire concerns, further evaluation of his foot became more positive. By the time Carolina hosted Pittsburgh three days later, the situation was much more optimistic. And when the Tar Heels traveled to Greensboro to host Notre Dame—a water-line break in Chapel Hill forced the game to be moved—Pinson went through very light pregame warmups with the team, although he still was not cleared to play.

The Tar Heels collected solid wins over the Panthers and the Irish, and the mood in the locker room noticeably improved.

"When everybody found out there was a good possibility Theo would be able to play, our moods changed," Berry said. "And his mood changed as well. He was able to be who he is, and support everyone and make everybody laugh. That lifted everybody up. We were able to continue to practice and know that everything would be just fine."

In fact, Pinson was able to play limited minutes in the February 9 game at Duke. But in the injury-riddled world of the 2017 Tar Heels, his return came just as Isaiah Hicks exited, tweaking his hamstring throwing down a dunk in practice. The senior estimated he was about 70 percent healthy on game night; he probably felt good enough to play if it had been an NCAA Tournament game, but there was still—even though it was Duke and Hicks' last trip to Cameron Indoor Stadium—a month until the postseason. The medical staff and coaches wanted to err on the side of caution.

Hicks' injury led to one of Williams' most fortuitous decisions of the season. With Pinson available, the Tar Heels could have just subbed Pinson for Hicks in the starting lineup. But Williams didn't want to rush Pinson back into big minutes, and he believed Luke Maye would ultimately be important to the team's success. The sophomore had played some mixed minutes in the nonconference portion of the schedule but hadn't quite yet found consistency.

With Hicks prone to foul trouble, however, there was a good chance

When everybody found out there was a good possibility Theo would be able to play, our moods changed. And his mood changed as well. We were able to continue to practice and know that everything would be just fine.

—JOEL BERRY II

Carolina's win over No. 6 Louisville
was one of five wins over top-10 teams.
(Photo by Jeffrey A. Camarati)

Maye's rebounding prowess would play a role in a key game in March or April. So as the day of the Duke game progressed, Maye seemed to be the likely choice to start.

Hicks had approached Maye earlier in the day. "I don't know if I'm going to be able to play," Hicks said to Maye. "You might have to start for me."

"No way, Isaiah," Maye said. "You can play. You're good."

But Williams knew better, and he decided Maye would get the start. He told the team—and Maye—while they went over the scouting report.

"It really showed me that my work ethic had been paying off," Maye said. "Looking back, that game definitely made me work harder. Coach Williams having the confidence to put me in my first career start in the biggest rivalry in college basketball really showed his thoughts on my game and how I could help the team. It gave me so much confidence for the rest of the year and helped me elevate my game to where it needed to be."

Despite a frustrating loss to Duke that night, Maye acquitted himself well in a tough environment, scoring eight points to go with two assists and zero turnovers in 20 minutes of action. As the Tar Heels entered the regular season's final month, Williams' team was gaining confidence and inching closer to full health for practically the first time in 2017.

Kennedy Meeks had 14 points, 10 boards, and two blocks in Carolina's 74–63 win over sixth-ranked Louisville. (Photo by Peyton Williams)

Senior Day is one of Roy Williams' favorite days of the season. It's also one of his most pressure-packed days.

Carolina's head coach becomes extremely invested in his players and their families. It starts during the recruiting process, when he consistently makes multiple trips to see a prospect and becomes acquainted with his family and the other important influences in his life.

It continues over the four years a player is at Carolina. In the modern era of college basketball, players who stay a full four years at their school can start to feel like Methuselah, as the rosters of other schools may turn over two or three times in that same stretch. Williams loves watching players grow both on and off the court, and he considers it his personal mission to ensure that every Tar Heel leaves Chapel Hill with a win in their last game in the Smith Center. In his history as a head coach at both Kansas and Carolina, his teams have lost just two games on Senior Day.

When he first came back to Chapel Hill from Lawrence, he spoke often—and glowingly—of the Senior Day ceremonies at Kansas. Flowers were thrown on the floor, speeches were made, standing ovations were given. Williams, who likes to say he's "corny as all get out," loved the tradition.

There have been some memorable Senior Days in Chapel Hill, too. Phil Ford had 34 points in his Senior Day win over Duke. Dean Smith started the tradition of starting every senior in their final home game, and Williams has continued it—even sending out six "starters" when the roster is senior-heavy to ensure all the veterans get to be on the floor for a brief moment at the outset.

But even with some big wins in the final home game of the year during the Williams era—including several that clinched an Atlantic Coast Conference regular-season championship—the Tar Heels struggled to get just the right mix of Senior Day pomp and circumstance. The program had tried senior speeches. It had tried videos. It had tried a mix of both.

And then, over the last two years, everything came together. The 2016 Senior Day, with Marcus Paige, Joel James, and Brice Johnson saying good-bye to the Smith Center crowd after a win over Syracuse, was nearly perfect. All three players had significantly matured during their stints at Carolina, and all three were able to express it perfectly. Johnson was the comic relief, James was the mature future leader, and then Paige brought it home while also bringing Williams to tears.

"I know one day I won't get to walk through this tunnel and meet with you at the beginning of practice every day," Paige said to Williams in front of the crowd after the game. "You've believed in me, and I can't thank you enough for that, because that allowed me to be a confident person and help me grow as a person. . . . I've tried to be every bit the player you wanted me to be, but

6

A SENIOR SENDOFF

Joel Berry led UNC past Duke with five three-pointers and 28 points.
(Photo by Peyton Williams)

Kennedy Meeks shared a pregame hug with his mom during Senior Night ceremonies. (Photo by Peyton Williams)

Carolina's seniors prior to the starting lineup being announced before the Duke game. (Photo by Jeffrey A. Camarati)

Justin Jackson became the 14th Tar Heel to capture ACC Player-of-the-Year honors. (Photo by Jeffrey A. Camarati)

you've also made me a better man. That's the most important thing. I'm ten times a better man than when I got here. Thank you."

The 2017 version of Senior Day carried even more intensity because it fell against Duke. Due largely to two key home wins over Virginia and Louisville, plus a road win at Pitt, the Tar Heels had already clinched a share of the ACC regular season title and the number one seed in the ACC Tournament. But a victory over the Blue Devils would earn an outright championship and would also send out the scholarship senior trio of Kennedy Meeks, Nate Britt, and Isaiah Hicks with a victory.

Hicks, who was never a fan of public speaking, gave a twist to the evening when he decided not to address the crowd on the microphone, instead doing it by video. It turned out to be the perfect finish for the Oxford native, who had struggled in recent games but exploded against Duke. At halftime, with Carolina holding a slim 48–46 lead, Justin Jackson told Hicks, "You're carrying us right now." Hicks went on to score 21 points to go with nine rebounds, one of the best performances of his career.

It was a fitting way for him to end his home tenure. The lifelong Tar Heel fan had been one of the easiest recruiting jobs of Williams' career. When his high school reputation began to explode, Hicks was contacted by schools

Joel Berry was one of four Tar Heels to reach 1,000 career points during the 2016–17 season. (Photo by Jeffrey A. Camarati)

around the country. Eventually, he barely paid attention to the letters that stuffed his mailbox. One day, though, was different.

"I was getting a lot of letters from people," Hicks said. "I wasn't paying attention to it. One day, my mom said, 'Guess where you got a letter from?' It was from Carolina. I was excited about that one, and we opened it together. Their letter said they had taken an interest in me and were looking forward to seeing me play more often. Once I got that letter, it was just a matter of time."

Assistant coach C. B. McGrath spearheaded Hicks' recruitment. Eventually, the entire Hicks family visited Chapel Hill and met with Williams. He offered Hicks a scholarship, which usually speeds the recruiting process but by no means finishes it. Hicks was different. The family had a drive of less than an hour home. By the time they arrived in Oxford, Hicks was ready to call and make his commitment.

Even though Britt was the lone member of the senior trio not from North Carolina, Williams still knew he had deep ties to Chapel Hill. The family had shown the coach a video of Britt made when he was much younger.

"He's sitting down on the floor with his knees up, cute as a button," Williams said. "He says, 'I want to go to North Carolina and play for Coach Roy Williams.'"

The most influential adult in Britt's life other than his parents was his grandfather, who lived in LaGrange, North Carolina. Every summer, Britt and his sister, Natalya, would spend a month with their grandfather. Ned Britt was strict, and the children spent much of their summer in church. When they weren't in church, Ned was often talking about his beloved Tar Heels, and Nate also adopted them as his favorite team.

"My dad would tease me and tell me I should get my own team," said Britt. "He told me I should root for Georgetown, since that's where I was from. But I always wanted Carolina to win."

Britt's family was extremely close-knit, and it gained a surrogate member with the addition of Kennedy Meeks. Britt was extremely reliable, the type of player whom, as Williams put it during the team's basketball banquet, he would go to when he needed something relayed to the team. That created a sort of odd-couple relationship with classmate Meeks, who sometimes bucked Williams' instructions and enjoyed his independence.

But the duo had an instant rapport—even if it developed in a unique fashion. During their freshman year, Britt and Meeks scuffled on one occasion in their dorm room. All three seniors—including Hicks, who was in the next room playing video games—agree it was the fault of J. P. Tokoto, a player one year older who had been tweaking both Hicks and Meeks.

Finally, the classmates agreed to settle it physically. It wasn't a heated, go-straight-at-each-other type of brawl. In fact, the combatants took the time

Justin Jackson scored eight first-half points as the Tar Heels built a 48–46 lead at the half over the Blue Devils on Senior Day. (Photo by J. D. Lyon Jr.)

Kennedy Meeks scored 1,482 career points and was one of only six Tar Heels to start in two NCAA title games. (Photo by Jeffrey A. Camarati)

Isaiah Hicks broke out of a scoring slump with
21 points against Duke in his final home game.
(Photo by Jeffrey A. Camarati)

to organize their room beforehand, moving the furniture out of the center of
the den to clear some space.

"J. P. kept egging it on," Meeks said. "Nate and I are so close we knew we
were going to be cool afterwards, no matter what happened. We laughed
about it at the end of the day, because it was pointless. We should've been
beating up on J. P. rather than beating up on each other. It definitely made
us grow closer as friends."

Humorously, what both Meeks and Britt remember best about the incident is the reaction of Hicks, the Oxford homebody who simply wanted to
peacefully play *Call of Duty*.

"All I remember, honestly, is Isaiah running out of the room in shock,"
Meeks said. "He was yelling, 'What are y'all doing?' I remember us being on
the ground looking up, and Isaiah was running out of the room."

The trio became very close. Hicks and Meeks were roommates all four
years at Carolina. Meeks and Britt became near-brothers. Britt was the one
who Williams rarely had to reprimand. Although his teammates claimed
he was not shy at all with them, Hicks was always the quiet one in public.
Choosing not to speak on Senior Day perfectly matched his personality.

While Meeks was usually quick with a joke, Hicks could make his teammates laugh just with his everyday actions. He sometimes wore two different

Justin Jackson scored 731 points in 2016–17, fifth-most in UNC history for one season. (Photo by Jeffrey A. Camarati)

socks. He was known for not always taking the time to put sheets on his bed, and if pizza was left in the kitchen for multiple weeks or spaghetti took up permanent residence in the oven, Hicks was probably responsible.

But Hicks was a sponge for Williams' coaching. The players laughed about an incident during the Louisville game, when Hicks was suffering through a 0-for-6 shooting stretch. A late turnover prompted Williams to remove Hicks from the game. On the bench, the coach shouted, "You're a great player! Play better than that! You can do better!"

It was one of the first times that Hicks, and not Meeks, had been the target of such an on-court explosion. McGrath tried to intervene. "OK, Coach, he's got it," McGrath said.

Hicks laughed when recounting the story. "That's when he drilled C. B. even harder than he was getting on me," he said with a grin.

"My biggest thing was that I was always listening to what Coach said," Hicks said. "I didn't want to take it as Coach just yelling at me or picking on me. I never wanted to get an attitude. If I get mad, I'll take it out on somebody on the court."

That wasn't always the approach taken by Meeks, who early in his UNC career could sometimes sulk when faced with adversity. He grew into a player who attempted to show some leadership. Before each game, it was Meeks who would gather the post players.

"We're the best big men in the country," he would tell his fellow centers and forwards. "We have to get out there and dominate these guys."

■ That's what they did against the Blue Devils on Senior Day. Hicks was sensational, and Meeks added eight points and eight rebounds. Carolina held a whopping 44–26 advantage on points in the paint, and Meeks capped off the evening with a vicious blocked shot against Duke post stalwart Amile Jefferson.

Even before the senior speeches began, the night had provided some of the very best of Carolina Basketball. Four of the six living players with retired jerseys were in the building—Lennie Rosenbluth, Phil Ford, Michael Jordan, and Antawn Jamison—and all four were feverishly cheering for the Tar Heels, with Jordan sprinkling in some occasional heckling of the game officials.

Jordan made an appearance at halftime, introducing the crowd to his Jordan Brand's partnership with the Tar Heel football team. He unintentionally uttered a phrase that would soon become a fan rallying cry for the 2017 team and launch multiple t-shirts: "The ceiling is the roof." It made very little sense, but that didn't matter, because it was Michael Jordan who'd said it. At the Smith Center, on Senior Day, with Carolina beating Duke, Jordan

> I was always listening to what Coach said. I didn't want to take it as Coach just yelling at me or picking on me. I never wanted to get an attitude. If I get mad, I'll take it out on somebody on the court.
>
> —ISAIAH HICKS

The Greatest of All Time, Michael Jordan, embraced Coach Williams following UNC's win over Duke. (Photo by Jeffrey A. Camarati)

could say whatever he wanted. That Michael Jordan could utter a halftime malaprop and then turn it into a sales bonanza for his own Jordan Brand was a perfect encapsulation of the sometimes wonderland-esque existence of the Tar Heel great.

As a general rule in the basketball world, it's very difficult to top an appearance by Michael Jordan. But this was Senior Day in Chapel Hill, and the 2017 event became just as heart-tugging as the 2016 edition. After the game, Britt and Meeks both took the microphone at center court in front of an appreciative Smith Center crowd.

Britt, still wearing his number-zero jersey, told the fans they had changed the way he thinks of himself.

Nate Britt gave an emotional speech to the crowd on Senior Night. (Photo by Jeffrey A. Camarati)

Carolina celebrated its eighth regular-season ACC title in Roy Williams' 14 years as
UNC's head coach. (Photo by J. D. Lyon Jr.)

Seniors Nate Britt and Kennedy Meeks became best friends over their four years in Chapel Hill. (Photo by J. D. Lyon Jr.)

"Coming from the area I'm from, when you're one of the better players, everyone roots against you," Britt said. "It's almost like everyone wants to see you fail. That's just the culture of our area. For me, that was motivation, because I've always wanted to try to prove people wrong. Wearing zero was a reminder that everyone thinks you're not good enough. It was a constant reminder I am trying to prove all of these people wrong.

"When I got to Carolina, I started to experience the other side of it. It was the first time I've heard so many times that I am someone's favorite player. With all the support and love that I've gotten the past four years, I don't think I can ever wear zero again. I think that would be wrong, because all of this support means I don't have to prove people wrong anymore."

Meeks took the microphone last. Teammates knew the emotional senior would have the toughest time getting through his speech, and he proved it by tearing up almost before he got started.

"One day," Meeks said, "I know Nate is going to be in my wedding." As the big man struggled to get through his speech, Britt came out to midcourt for a quick hug, once again being a big brother to Meeks. Few realized that when Britt's grandfather passed away during Britt's sophomore year, it was Meeks who tracked him down in the Smith Center and was there when Britt couldn't stop crying. The next night, Britt scored his career high of 17 points.

It was fitting, then, that Britt and Meeks would go out together on Senior Day, one last Chapel Hill experience for a duo that had been through plenty. Over on the Tar Heel bench sat Roy Williams, alternating between laughter and tears as the stories and speeches flowed. This was Senior Day exactly as he'd always imagined it. Two years in a row, the day had showcased the very best of Carolina Basketball, of players maturing and forming new relationships and, don't forget, winning together. The Tar Heels felt they had given away the earlier Duke game in Durham. This time, it didn't get away.

"It was something we wanted to do not just for ourselves, but also for our fellow classmates and Chapel Hill in general," said Joel Berry II, who was sensational in hitting five-of-five three-pointers in the first half and then closing with seven points in the final 4:28. "That game was bigger than us. We wanted to give ourselves something to celebrate, and we wanted to give the students something to celebrate."

The entire program had something to celebrate. In a year when national observers trumpeted the Atlantic Coast Conference as perhaps the best basketball conference in history, the Tar Heels won the league by two games. It was Carolina's eighth regular-season title in Williams' 14 years as head coach; no other school or coach had more than three regular-season championships in that span.

"I'm really proud of that," Williams said. "I want the volume of work for three months to be important. Three days in the ACC Tournament are not as important to me as what we do for three months. I always want to enjoy three months more than I enjoy three days. The satisfaction of doing it over a long time means you're having a heck of a year."

"I was mad," Roy Williams said frankly.

He's talking about the locker room scene in Brooklyn's Barclays Center after Carolina's 93–83 ACC Tournament semifinal loss to Duke. One day earlier, the Tar Heels had exorcised some regular-season demons with a 78–53 thrashing of Miami. The game was a clinical dissection of a Hurricanes team that had dismantled Carolina in Coral Gables while UNC was reeling from Theo Pinson's second injury.

Just a week removed from beating Duke in the Smith Center, it looked like the Tar Heels were set up to beat the Blue Devils again, win the season series, and move on to play for the ACC Tournament title for the third straight year.

Instead, Carolina squandered a 49–42 halftime lead, saw Mike Krzyzewski's team blitz them by 17 points in the second half, and were left to listen to rampant national speculation that perhaps the loss had cost them a number-one regional seed in the upcoming NCAA Tournament.

Fans moaned about Duke's 37 free-throw attempts and about major foul trouble for Joel Berry. Williams didn't want to hear about it. As soon as his team reached the locker room, he blistered them—not for the loss, but for the way they had played in the loss.

"I didn't think we played as hard as Duke did or as intelligently as Duke did," Williams said. "I think we were still feeling good about beating them in the Smith Center. I was not going to accept that kind of play. I was not going to accept that Duke got down on the floor for a loose ball better than we did, that we didn't guard them. Because I thought not only did they do everything better than we did, but they wanted it more than us. That really ticked me off."

He made it clear to his team that he was ticked off, then he stormed out of the locker room. Most of the players sat silently.

Williams stormed into the coaches' locker room. A few minutes passed. Then he walked back into the players' locker room, this time with a new message. This one was no less passionate, but it had a different tone. Outside, in the hallways and in the stands and on the playing floor of the Barclays Center, the ACC Tournament continued. Williams wanted to refocus his team on what was next for them.

"I had to tell them it was a bump in the road," Williams said. "It was a bump in the road I did not appreciate, but it doesn't mean our season stopped. If we play that way, our season will be over. But look at what we've done in the past. We've won national championships at North Carolina twice when we lost in the ACC semifinals. I wanted to chew their butts out, tell them how disappointed and mad I was, but also give them that apple in front of them. We could still do what we wanted to do."

7
BOARD WORK

Stilman White and the Tar Heels turned the tables on Miami with a 25-point win in the ACC Tournament. (Photo by Jim Hawkins)

Theo Pinson's dunk wasn't enough as Duke rallied to beat UNC in Brooklyn in the ACC semifinals. (Photo by Jim Hawkins)

■ The next day, the Tar Heels started moving toward what they still wanted to achieve. While Duke and Notre Dame stayed in Brooklyn to play for the ACC Tournament title on Saturday night, the Tar Heels left Saturday morning to return home, the players wearing the suits they had probably packed with the intention of wearing to the championship game. By the time they arrived home, there were approximately 30 hours remaining before the NCAA Tournament brackets would be announced. Williams had plenty to accomplish with his team before he could feel comfortable entering NCAA play.

His work began in the film room in the Smith Center locker room. The entire locker-room complex had been renovated over the summer through the generosity of Rams Club donors. The Tar Heels now watched film in a plush theater, with comfortable seats for every player and a huge projection screen.

That gave them a clear view of exactly what their head coach wanted them to see. Berry had earned his fourth foul against Duke with 15:04 left in the game. At that point, Carolina had an eight-point advantage. Berry compli-

Isaiah Hicks scored 38 points in UNC's two ACC Tournament games. (Photo by J. D. Lyon Jr.)

cated the foul issues by showing frustration on the bench, and Williams let him sit there until 4:58 remained and Duke had built a seven-point lead.

At the Barclays Center, during the flow of the game, Berry had been insistent that he was the victim of bad calls by the officiating crew. Back at the Smith Center, though, he fell victim to one of Williams' very favorite sayings: "The eye in the sky don't lie."

That's why the Carolina coach ran the video back and forth multiple times in front of the team. Berry was especially miffed about his third foul, a reach-in against Duke point guard Frank Jackson less than two minutes into the second half.

Williams cued up the video. There was Berry, reaching across Jackson's body.

"You can't have two fouls and make a silly reach foul," Williams said. "I went back and forth in slow motion and told him, 'You did foul. Don't come running over to me and say you didn't touch him. You did foul. There it is.' I

The thing that drove us last year was that we were having so much fun, and we enjoyed the journey so much. I wanted us to do anything it took not to lose, so we could keep going and have this journey with each other.

—THEO PINSON

ran it back and forth ten times to show him. So don't give me those excuses and blame it on the officials. You made the mistake."

But the team meeting wasn't just about Berry. Williams took a black marker and walked to the white board in the film room. On the board, he wrote seven features he believed made the 2017 Tar Heels successful. Then he highlighted four of them, which he believed the Tar Heels had done especially poorly in Brooklyn: guarding the ball defensively, boxing out and rebounding, running both ways, and talking to each other. The message stayed on the board throughout the postseason and lingered into the summer, a reminder of the success the Tar Heels achieved with a focus on the details.

"Coach challenged us," said Kennedy Meeks. "Once he wrote that on the board, all of us took a look at it and realized how important the rest of the season was. We didn't want to lose again. I think that was always in the back of everyone's minds."

"These are the major goals we always talk about," Williams told his team. "Focus on these four."

"That really got us back into it," said Isaiah Hicks. "We knew what it takes to get there."

In Brooklyn, it had been Williams who tried to ignite his team with a pointed message. Back in Chapel Hill, it was Theo Pinson. He stood up and addressed the team. Often, his comments were tinged with humor. This time, it was pure emotion.

"We can win this," he told them. "I don't want our last game together to be the first or second game of the tournament. I don't get to play with Isaiah, and Nate, and Kennedy, and Stilman, and Kanler ever again after this. Let's just go win it. I want to be able to go to the very last day with you guys, and I want us to enjoy this together for as long as we can."

"I wanted to bring back the point of last year," Pinson said when reflecting on his message. "The thing that drove us last year was that we were having so much fun, and we enjoyed the journey so much. That drove us not to lose. I wanted us to do anything it took not to lose, so we could keep going and have this journey with each other. That was my main point. Play for each other and do everything you can so we can keep this train moving.

"We knew everything Coach wrote on the board. It's what we had been taught all year. It was just a little reminder, and we had to go out and do it."

The off-court motivation helped Carolina start over on the court. In addition to practice, the players spent much of Sunday watching highlights of Duke celebrating the ACC Tournament title. The most popular national storyline regarding the NCAA Tournament field was whether the Blue Devils or Tar Heels would receive a top regional seed. There was little doubt that Carolina had the more impressive season-long credentials. But there was

The Tar Heels were ecstatic when CBS announced the team had secured a top seed in the NCAA Tournament. (Photo by Josh Reavis)

also little doubt that Duke had the momentum after winning two of the three head-to-head meetings.

As usual, the Tar Heels gathered at Williams' home to watch the selection show. The players and coaches sat around the television. Players think of the unveiling of the brackets more like the fans do, focusing on matchups and individuals. Coaches tend to think of the brackets in terms of scouting: who have we seen, who do we know, and where can we get the tape?

Williams is the default bracketologist, even though he professes to spend less time than anyone in the room evaluating seeds or regions. Players ask him what he thinks about a certain seed, or about who might get in or be left out. Carolina alum Kenny Smith is on the nationally televised selection show, and Williams and Smith have been known to exchange texts during commercial breaks in the broadcast, bantering about Charles Barkley's latest comment or other show hijinks.

The drama disappeared fairly quickly, as Duke was announced as the two seed in the East Region, meaning Carolina had almost certainly earned a one seed. The CBS graphic listing the Tar Heels prompted a big cheer in the Williams living room, and then the team had to sit and wait to find out who the other 15 teams were in the South Region.

Carolina's 2017 national title bore several striking resemblances to some of the program's other championships. But in one way, this year's team was an anomaly.

The 2017 Tar Heels had three North Carolina natives in the starting lineup: Theo Pinson, Kennedy Meeks, and Isaiah Hicks. The program's five other NCAA champions combined had just four starters who were natives of the Tar Heel State, and that's counting Michael Jordan—who was born in Brooklyn but raised in Wilmington—as a North Carolina native.

The 1957 team was dominated by New Yorkers, with head coach Frank McGuire organizing a New York–to–Chapel Hill pipeline that resulted in an undefeated record and triple-overtime championship defeat of Wilt Chamberlain and Kansas. The 1982 club had Jordan and Gastonia's James Worthy, and the 1993 Tar Heels had Garner's Donald Williams. But Roy Williams' previous two title teams had just one North Carolinian in the starting lineup.

Before he returned to Carolina in 2003, Williams had established deep recruiting roots in the western half of the country, where players were more receptive to Kansas recruiting pitches. His national recruiting reach has given the Tar Heels an even broader net to cast; the 2005 team had Marvin Williams from the state of Washington, and Missouri's Tyler Hansbrough was the centerpiece of the 2009 team.

But Williams reminded his staff in recent years that North Carolina was also a fertile area for prep talent. Of course, that didn't always mean the recruiting pitch was easy. Oxford's Isaiah Hicks was a lifelong Tar Heel fan, but Charlotte's Kennedy Meeks and Greensboro's Theo Pinson were—"Don't hate me for this," Meeks says—childhood Duke fans.

Despite his early and misguided love for the team with the darker shade of blue, Pinson had actually attended his first Carolina game at the age of eight.

Carolina's senior class included North Carolina natives Isaiah Hicks and Kennedy Meeks, who started on the front line and played pivotal roles in UNC winning the national title. (Photo by Jim Hawkins)

Even a decade later, he remembered the details of his first exposure to the Tar Heels. "My first time in the Smith Center, Carolina was playing Winston-Salem State," he said. "I was amazed. I remember thinking, 'Wow, this place is pretty cool.'" He also attended a Carolina-Texas game in his hometown of Greensboro; being shelved with an injury was even more painful for him when the 2017 Carolina–Notre Dame game was moved to his hometown because of a Chapel Hill water emergency.

Being local helped in his recruitment; his mother had developed a love for Sean May, and Pinson fondly remembered watching Danny Green, Ty Lawson, and the rest of the 2009 champions.

Playing close to home was an important

Hicks, Jackson, Berry, Pinson, and Meeks went 11–2 as starters, including all six games in the NCAA Tournament.
(Photo by Jack Morton)

consideration for Meeks, who relished the opportunity for his younger siblings to have frequent opportunities to see him play in person. His younger sister had a simple message for Meeks before every game. "Dominate," she told him, a message he would then relay to Joel Berry in their pre-tip-off ritual.

"Growing up as a North Carolina kid, you understand how important Tar Heel basketball is to everyone," Pinson said. "This is something people talk about all day, every day, and we're so lucky to get to be part of it in this way. Being a Tar Heel is something that matters to everyone in this state."

Each player and staff member likely had at least one or two opponents they did not want to see in Carolina's bracket. At that time of year, every possible foe has the ability to end the season. Every team is capable, and so every team seems dangerous.

One Tar Heel, though, harbored a hope for an opponent he *did* want to see, and it was probably the same one several others wanted to avoid: Kentucky.

Ever since he'd gone to dinner with Berry after the game in Las Vegas, Pinson had been hoping the Tar Heels would face the Wildcats again. The two squads were clearly two of the best teams in the country, and the marquee pedigrees of both would have made for an excellent Final Four or national championship matchup.

Instead, the Wildcats were placed as the second seed in the South, setting up a potential regional final showdown. As soon as they appeared in the bracket, Pinson bounced out of his chair, clapping and cheering. He'd missed the first meeting. He wasn't going to miss this one, if it happened.

"I think I was the only one who cheered when Kentucky was in our bracket," Pinson said. "I was hoping we'd see them again. Everybody was like, 'Why are you cheering?' I said, 'Don't y'all see who is in our bracket?' I was hoping we'd play them the entire time."

After all 68 teams were revealed, Williams muted the television and addressed his team. "I stood here in August, and I told you there was a team in this room good enough to win a national championship," he said. "I believe that in my body and soul."

Williams then outlined the schedule for early in the week before the team would be required to depart for Greenville, S.C., for pretournament practice and media obligations. "You'll go to class on Wednesday, and then we'll leave Wednesday night," he said.

Justin Jackson raised his hand. "Coach," he said, "it's spring break."

"Is it really?" Williams asked. A cheer went up in the room—the players celebrating because they had a week free from class and the coaches because spring break meant a much-easier-to-navigate schedule.

The players scarfed down the last of the brownies and ice cream available in the Williams kitchen and dispersed. The coaching staff gathered in the living room and talked strategy for the week. Steve Robinson suggested spending a practice period or two working on zone defense, not as a change to Carolina's fundamental approach but as a fallback in case of foul trouble or a hot-shooting opponent.

The group discussed Jackson's play in Brooklyn, where he had shot 5-for-18 from the three-point line and for the first time all season looked like he was forcing his offense. Watching it on film, he looked like a different player over the past week than the one who had earned ACC-Player-of-the-Year

Freshman Shea Rush made fedoras for each of the players and coaches that were worn throughout the run to the national title. (Photo by J. D. Lyon Jr.)

honors—and that award was precisely what the coaches speculated could be the problem.

Jackson had been extremely hard on himself after the loss to Duke, repeatedly telling the media he was responsible for the loss. For the final month of the season, most observers believed the ACC Player-of-the-Year race had come down to Jackson and Duke's Luke Kennard. (Wake Forest's John Collins actually finished second, with Notre Dame's Bonzie Colson third; Jackson received 24 votes to Kennard's five.) In the last four games, including two against Kennard, Jackson was 7-for-31 from three-point range. He looked

(L) One of Greenville's finest shows off his affinity for the Tar Heels. (Photo by J. D. Lyon Jr.)

(R) South Carolina native Seventh Woods signs autographs for fans in Greenville. (Photo by J. D. Lyon Jr.)

like a player who was trying to justify winning ACC Player of the Year rather than one who knew he'd earned it.

Williams told his staff he'd meet with the junior. It turned out someone had beaten him to it.

"My first conversation came with my parents right after we lost to Duke," Jackson said. "My mom told me, 'You don't have to live up to being ACC Player of the Year. You were Player of the Year because of what you did throughout the season and the type of player that you are. So don't worry about being the Player of the Year. Be the best Justin Jackson you can be.' When she said that, that helped a lot."

As usual, Sharon Jackson was right. Williams reinforced the message in his office before the team left for Greenville.

"We had a nice meeting," Williams said. "We talked about who he had to please. He had to please himself, and he had to please me, and other than that, don't worry about anyone else. What are you trying to prove? Are they going to give you two ACC Player-of-the-Year awards? Or are they going to take it away from you if you don't prove it? I stressed to him that he didn't have to do anything different than what he did during the regular season, because in the ACC Tournament, I did think he tried to be different."

"Once I got the award, I felt like I had to show people why I got it and why Luke didn't get it," Jackson said. "That's human nature. It's hard not to get

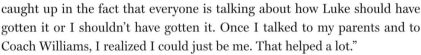

(L) Carolina routed Texas Southern by 39 points in the first round of the NCAA Tournament. (Photo by J. D. Lyon Jr.)

(R) Joel Berry made only one field goal against Texas Southern and turned his ankle late in the game. (Photo by Robert Crawford)

caught up in the fact that everyone is talking about how Luke should have gotten it or I shouldn't have gotten it. Once I talked to my parents and to Coach Williams, I realized I could just be me. That helped a lot."

It wasn't just Jackson who had a better outlook. The entire Tar Heel team was loose and confident going into Greenville. Shea Rush gave each player and coach a handmade hat before the team's departure. The squad decided to wear them on the road trip and sported them on the plane on Wednesday, and again with their suits and ties when the team went out to a pregame dinner at Greenville's renowned Hall's Chophouse. Rush had customized each hat for the recipient, even the three players he said were most hesitant— Seventh Woods, Isaiah Hicks, and Jackson. But with 12 players fully committed, the other three quickly joined the group. "I'm not a hat person," Woods said. "But once I put it on, I kind of fell in love."

Jackson, meanwhile, emerged from his brief slump. The immediate wit-

Senior Kanler Coker ignited the Tar Heel bench (see opposite) with a reverse layup against Texas Southern. (Photo by J. D. Lyon Jr.)

ness to his improved mindset was 16-seed Texas Southern. The junior scored 19 points in the first half and drained five of his eight three-point attempts, setting the program's single-season three-pointer mark in the process. Carolina was unquestionably more gifted and talented than the Tigers, but Jackson was also unquestionably in a better rhythm. His five three-pointers—which all came in the first half—tied the mark for the third-most trifectas ever made by a Tar Heel in an NCAA Tournament game.

The game, a 103–64 whipping, was never really in doubt. The biggest issue came in the second half, when Berry went down with an apparent twisted ankle. The Tar Heels had just showed in Brooklyn that they struggled when he left the floor. That game had emphasized the stark reality: Carolina was good enough to advance in the NCAA Tournament without Berry, but they were not good enough to win the national title without him.

The Tar Heels were a loose and confident group throughout the 2017 NCAA Tournament run. (Photo by J. D. Lyon Jr.)

On the UNC bench, athletics trainer Doug Halverson asked Berry an interesting question: "What do you need to do to feel like you're OK?"

Berry told him he wanted to get back onto the court, even though the game was decided, and get a couple minutes of playing time to confirm he could run and cut. He stayed in for 3:58, missed the only shot he took, but gained some confidence that he could play on the injury.

"When I started getting up and down the court, I forgot about my ankle," Berry said. Nationally, Berry's ankle was mostly just a footnote. Inside the team, however, it would be the dominant storyline of the next 36 hours.

On Sunday evening, the Tar Heels straggled through the hallways of Bon Secours Wellness Arena, heading for the team bus that would take them back to the Greenville airport for the return trip to Chapel Hill.

Just looking at some of their faces, it was hard to tell exactly what had transpired in the round-of-32 NCAA Tournament game against Arkansas. They looked exhausted. Several players sat on the bus while they awaited the arrival of Roy Williams so the team could depart.

"Man," said Theo Pinson, looking at his teammates. "That game took everything. Literally everything we had."

At the moment, no one was entirely sure what had just happened. The Tar Heels were still alive—they knew that because Williams had written a big "16" on the white board in the locker room after the game. At the time, there was no context. There was just the exhaustion of what they knew was a mammoth comeback to survive the Razorbacks, 72–65.

The final seven-point margin was deceptive. Carolina had raced to an early 30–13 advantage but led by just five points at halftime. Arkansas took the lead seven minutes into the second half and held a 65–60 lead with just 3:28 remaining, putting Carolina on the verge of elimination just one day after 2016 national champion Villanova—the number-one seed in the East Regional—was sent home by Wisconsin.

Tar Heel basketball history is littered with program-defining comebacks. The signature game came in 1974 against Duke, when Dean Smith's Tar Heels rallied from eight points down with only 17 seconds remaining at Carmichael Auditorium, doing it without the benefit of the three-point line. In 1993, a good Florida State team led UNC by 21 points with under 12 minutes remaining and was up by 19 points with nine minutes left. Smith again engineered an unforgettable comeback, this time with George Lynch sealing the rally with a steal and two-handed thunder dunk.

But both of those games happened during the regular season. In the entire history of Carolina Basketball, in the 158 NCAA Tournament games the program had played prior to March 19, 2017, the Tar Heels had never trailed by a larger deficit with less time on the clock and still won the game.

At the time, of course, the players and coaches didn't realize that daunting historical fact. And so, with under four minutes to play, Williams made one of the most important decisions of the season. It wasn't based on analytics or data or statistics. It was based purely on reading the looks on his players' faces.

"In any other game this year, I never saw the looks on their faces that I saw in the Arkansas game," Williams said.

The look was fear. And so, in the great tradition of Smith—who was prone to saying, "Isn't this going to be fun?" when his team was trailing and facing

8

THE COMEBACK

Roy Williams upped his record to 76–24 in NCAA Tournament play after UNC's six wins in the 2017 Tournament. (Photo by Jim Hawkins)

97

Carolina's win over Arkansas sent the Tar Heels to the Sweet 16 for the ninth time under Roy Williams. (Photo by J. D. Lyon Jr.)

a tough situation—Williams chose an encouraging approach in the Carolina huddle.

"We had to do something to get the momentum changed," Williams said. "I decided to go 180 degrees and told them, 'This is going to be great. We haven't won a game like this all year. This is going to help us later on, too. All we have to do is play. We do this all the time in practice.'"

The Tar Heels regularly have a period of practice devoted to trailing 86–80 late in the game. This wasn't much different.

"I decided to do that because I didn't like the looks on their faces," Williams said. "I thought it had to be something different instead of, 'Dadgummit, why are we doing this or you guys have to start doing that!'"

His approach was a major departure from his normal strategy at that point in the game, and it took at least one player by surprise.

"He said, 'We haven't won a game like this all year,'" Theo Pinson said. "And I was like, 'Why would you say that?' And then he said, 'We might as well do it right now. We don't have a choice.'"

Kennedy Meeks had 16 points in the second round win over the Razorbacks in Greenville. (Photo by J. D. Lyon Jr.)

Carolina held Arkansas scoreless over the final 3:27 and ended the game on a 12–0 run. (Photo by Jim Hawkins)

Isaiah Hicks was one of the first players to speak up. "I'm not going out like this!" the senior shouted in the huddle.

"Coach told us we were going to win the game," said Joel Berry II. "But he said we had to believe we were going to win the game. And that if we did everything he told us to do, we would win. He tells us that all the time, but at that time it meant way more than a regular-season game because if we lose that one, we're done for the rest of the season.

"I looked down the bench, and you could see everybody looking right into Coach's eyes. Usually you have guys who are tying their shoes, looking for water, or grabbing towels—but at that time it was like Coach had grabbed something in our body and made us pay attention to him. We went out on the court and everybody just changed."

On the way back to the court, the five Tar Heels on the floor—Berry, Jackson, Hicks, Pinson, and Kennedy Meeks—paused for a quick huddle.

"Save nothing," Pinson told them. "Leave it all out here right now."

"We're going to win this game," Berry said. "No matter what, we're going to win this game."

"We all believed it," Pinson said. "We just knew we had to make the plays."

The key play came after Berry sank a pair of free throws to trim the Arkansas lead to 65–62. The Razorbacks missed a three-pointer with under 2:30 remaining. Thirty seconds earlier, Hicks had corralled an offensive rebound but gone back up to the rim too softly, and Hog big man Moses Kingsley forcefully swatted the ball into the UNC bench.

This time down, Carolina took advantage of Kingsley's aggressiveness. The Tar Heels called "slip," which had become a signature Jackson-to-Hicks play out of the secondary break. Hicks threw a seemingly innocuous pass to Jackson on the left wing, then jogged toward the ACC Player of the Year, apparently intending to set a ball screen to free the sharpshooter for a possible game-tying three-pointer.

Three Arkansas defenders reacted as though that was the move they expected. But just before he set his feet to set a screen, Hicks made a quick cut to the basket. Jackson delivered a perfect pass that led him just enough, and Hicks caught the ball with only one defender having a chance to make a play on the ball: Kingsley.

"I saw Moses down there and he had just blocked my shot into the bench," Hicks said. "I thought, 'He's not doing that any more. If I catch this ball, I'm dunking it.' And that's what happened."

It did indeed. Hicks took off outside the lane and soared to the rim, absorbing some contact from Kingsley while slamming through a huge dunk. The Tar Heel bench exploded, and the deficit was now just one point.

"When we called 'slip,' that was a really big moment," Pinson said. "We needed that play to work. We knew they wouldn't be ready for it, and we

Isaiah Hicks and Justin Jackson sparked UNC's late defensive surge that helped prevent a second-round upset. (Photo by Robert Crawford)

needed Isaiah to finish. Once it worked, I was like, 'OK, we're about to win this game.' I knew we were about to get a stop. We just needed to execute."

Pinson's energy was bubbling over, and he was boisterous as he got back on defense.

"I think I saw him slap the floor," Hicks said with a grin. "I was like, 'That dude never does that.' It reminded me of during AAU ball when guys try to provide energy by slapping the floor or picking up full-court. Once I saw him do that, I was like, 'Let's go.' Everybody started moving defensively, and I felt that really affected them. We had this whole body of energy."

Arkansas missed another jumper, and Hicks pulled down the rebound in

Joel Berry thought he was done when he rolled his left ankle on a drive to the lane in the NCAA South Regional Final against Kentucky. He was in so much pain he thought his day had ended without a real chance to send Carolina back to the Final Four.

That only added to the troubles Berry's ankles had been giving him recently. A week earlier, in the second half of the win over Texas Southern in Greenville, South Carolina, Berry had landed on another player's foot and sprained his right ankle. He later returned but couldn't practice the next day. He acknowledged the ankle was still painful but downplayed it to the media. "I feel fine, it's still a little sore," Berry told reporters while estimating his condition at 75 or 80 percent.

Still, UNC's medical team—athletics trainer Doug Halverson, strength and conditioning coordinator Jonas Sahratian, orthopedist Dr. Alex Creighton, physician Dr. Tom Brickner, and chiropractor Dr. Todd Staker—wasn't satisfied.

"We did our best to manage and treat Joel, but we didn't want to wake up on Sunday and wish, 'Man I wish we'd done more,'" Halverson said. "We made some improvements during the day, but Joel still had lingering symptoms. It was luck that we were close enough to someone we knew and trusted."

The group arranged for Berry to make the 100-mile trip from Greenville to Charlotte to see Dr. Nevin Markel on Saturday night before Sunday's game against the Razorbacks.

"Dr. Markel is a chiropractor and the best soft-tissue guy in Charlotte," said Sahratian, who has also referred former Tar Heels Marvin Williams and Tyler Hansbrough to Markel as professional players for the Charlotte Hornets.

Markel used a number of techniques to treat Berry's ankle that were unavailable to the UNC doctors in Greenville, and afterward the point guard had no doubt that the trip was worthwhile.

Jonas Sahratian (second from left) and Doug Halverson (right) helped Joel Berry rehab after he sprained an ankle in the first round of the NCAA Tournament. (Photo by J. D. Lyon Jr.)

"On the ride back I just knew that I had my confidence back," Berry said. "I just had that bounce back to me, and it was something that I needed."

Berry gutted out 10 points in 34 painful minutes the next day against Arkansas. The ankle sprain turned out to be relatively minor, and five days later, he was at his best, leading the Tar Heels with an NCAA Tournament career-high 26 points in the Sweet 16 win over Butler.

Trouble returned in practice the next day when Berry tweaked the right ankle by stepping on Kennedy Meeks' foot. It was another relatively minor sprain, but one with another short recovery window before playing Kentucky.

Berry was ready to go against the Wildcats, but frustration returned when he landed awkwardly and sprained his *other* ankle less than five minutes into the game. Accompanied by Halverson, he hobbled in pain

Joel Berry played 35 minutes against Oregon and 37 against Gonzaga despite a pair of sprained ankles. (Photo by J. D. Lyon Jr.)

to the locker room, where he was able to cut, run, and skip on the ankle—but only while wincing in pain and shedding a few tears.

"I thought that was it," he said. "I thought I wasn't going to be able to play anymore the rest of the tournament. And I just went back to the locker room and told myself, 'You can't let your team down.'"

"He had to decide, could he work through the pain," Halverson said. "That was a moment when you saw his toughness find a new level because he had to push through discomfort that many athletes wouldn't have been able to do."

Berry returned to the court and eventually played 33 minutes, scoring 11 points on some tough drives to the basket. After the game, he needed assistance getting off the ladder after cutting his celebratory piece of the nets.

The ankles were a key topic of conversation heading into the Final Four. In fact, potential in-flight ankle swelling helped push the Tar Heels to leave for Phoenix a day early to allow an extra day to recover.

Berry was able to practice only twice on a restricted basis in Arizona, but he scored 11 points in 35 minutes against Oregon.

"The semifinal game was the first chance Joel really had to test the ankle in crowded, full-contact situations because he'd been limited in practice," Halverson said. "By the championship game, he'd gained some confidence to help him be more aggressive."

A more-assertive Berry hit four three-pointers and scored a game-high 22 points with a team-high six assists in 37 minutes in the national title game win over Gonzaga. Final Four Most Outstanding Player honors followed.

"I did it for my teammates, and my thought process the whole time was that I'm not giving up on them," Berry said. "It was nothing for myself. It wasn't anything else but going out there and just fighting for the guys that I love and the guys that I love competing with."

Coach always tells us, "When the shot goes up, try to get in front of the defender," because you have an easier rebound that way. So that's what I did.

—KENNEDY MEEKS

traffic. He was fouled, and went to the free-throw line for a one-and-one opportunity with 1:44 left.

There was a time in Hicks' career when he would have been the last Tar Heel anyone would have wanted at the line. He made just 57.9 percent of his free throws as a freshman and was a barely improved 62.1 percent as a sophomore. But his percentage leaped to 75.6 percent as a junior, and he finished his senior campaign at 78.6 percent.

He didn't make a miraculous mechanical adjustment. He just matured, spent significant extra time working on his charity tosses, and made a conscious change to his mental approach. Instead of focusing on the result, he focused on the process. He no longer bounced the ball at the line while worrying if the ball would go through the net. Instead, he found a process that worked, followed it every time, and trusted that his routine would pay dividends.

It did, and Hicks drained both shots, giving Carolina the lead for the first time since the score was 46–45. Arkansas had held the lead for over eleven minutes; they would not lead again.

"I just wasn't willing to go out like that," Hicks said after the game, echoing his proclamation in the Tar Heel huddle.

Then it was time for another senior who wasn't ready for his career to end. With under 90 seconds to play, Meeks recorded a blocked shot on the defensive end. Then, after Berry drove the lane with the shot clock winding down and ran into traffic on his way to the rim, Meeks warded off Kingsley and tipped the ball back in with his left hand to provide a three-point advantage.

The play wasn't particularly fancy, which made it a good fit for Meeks. But it also wasn't as lucky as it might have appeared upon first glance. While the play was running, it looked like the Tar Heel center had just happened to swat at the ball and redirect it through the rim. In reality, Williams coaches his post men to work on tip-ins. At that point in the season, the Tar Heels had held 92 practices. In 46 of those practices, they had worked on tip-ins.

Even as he saw Berry driving to the rim, Meeks could hear Williams in his head.

"Coach always tells us, 'When the shot goes up, try to get in front of the defender,' because you have an easier rebound that way," Meeks said. "So that's what I did." It was a textbook example of a seemingly minor point of emphasis by Williams in practice paying off on the biggest stage.

Fittingly, the offensive rebound was the 999th of Meeks' UNC career. He recorded his 1,000th on a defensive board that preserved the three-point advantage, making him just the ninth Tar Heel ever to reach quadruple figures in rebounds.

Hicks made another couple of free throws to seal the game, and then

Justin Jackson's dunk with seconds to play capped
UNC's win that sent the Tar Heels to the Sweet 16.
(Photo by J. D. Lyon Jr.)

Jackson iced it with a dunk. The furious comeback was over, capped with what eventually became a 12–0 run to finish the game.

The players and coaches sprinted to the locker room for one of the most jubilant postgame celebrations of the season. In the moment, they hadn't had time to consider how they were making the comeback. It was just a missed shot there, a rebound here, a timely basket there.

Afterward, though, Williams considered what happened.

"Our defense was really good," he said. "And the pressure got to them. My team was more positive than their team was. They were shocked that they were losing the lead, which made their next shot tougher, and the next shot tougher, and the turnover easier, and the free throws tougher. Even though we were behind, we were much more positive than they were. They were just trying to hold on."

The win instantly went onto a very short list of momentous Carolina comebacks in the NCAA Tournament. There were only three that were comparable.

In 1977, Dean Smith engineered a recovery from five points down with 5:54 to play against Notre Dame on St. Patrick's Day. Phil Ford scored 29 points and made four clutch free throws in the final minute, including a pair in the final two seconds to seal the win.

In 2000, during Bill Guthridge's remarkable run to the Final Four, Carolina trailed Tennessee by seven points with 4:48 remaining. But the Tar Heels ended the game on a 15–3 run, sparked by Ed Cota and Joseph Forte.

The only example of a similar NCAA Tournament comeback in the Roy Williams era came in 2014. Playing in San Antonio, Carolina was down by five points with 4:23 left and was having serious problems defending Providence guard Bryce Cotton. But Marcus Paige tied the game on a three-pointer with 1:06 remaining, and then James Michael McAdoo—a 54 percent free-throw shooter for the season—made a pair of free throws and grabbed a key offensive rebound, all in the final 3.5 seconds, to clinch the win.

The win over the Razorbacks was essential, of course, because it prolonged the season. But Tar Heel players felt it also mattered because it changed a mindset.

"It was a blessing because we were able to move on to the next game," said Jackson. "It also ended up helping us for later games down the road. Honestly, there is no way we should have beaten Arkansas. There is no way we should have won it. But figuring out a way to win helped us figure out how to win against Kentucky, and against Oregon, and against Gonzaga."

Williams has long told his teams that every drive to the national title contains at least one miraculous escape. The 1957 team won back-to-back triple overtime games in the Final Four. The 1982 team had to outlast James Madison. The 1993 squad survived a missed potentially game-winning dunk.

In 2005, Raymond Felton's foul trouble meant the Tar Heels had to struggle past pesky Villanova. And in 2009, Carolina received a tougher-than-expected game against LSU in the second round.

Every year, potential champions fall in games just like the one the Tar Heels had just played against Arkansas. Talent has become so widespread in college basketball that with the one-and-out format, every single March game is dangerous. None of the previous three biggest tournament comebacks had led to a national title. As the bus left Greenville, however, the Tar Heels were one of just 16 teams remaining that still had a chance.

"From that point on, we knew if we listened to Coach and bought into what he's doing and what he wants us to do, we were going to get where we wanted to be," said Berry. "It changed our whole season."

The two wins in Greenville earned the Tar Heels a berth in Memphis, one of Roy Williams' favorite cities. It didn't have the beauty of Maui, but it had three key factors to earn Williams' appreciation.

First, Carolina had a good history there. The Tar Heels went through Memphis on the way to the 2009 championship, thumping Gonzaga and then overpowering Oklahoma and Blake Griffin. Williams identifies cities not by their TripAdvisor rating but by their relationship to UNC wins. On that account, Memphis was a winner.

Second, the city had good barbecue. Williams' travel philosophy is pretty simple: find a winner and stick with it. He'd been eating ribs at Memphis's famous Rendezvous restaurant for most of his coaching career. He had become so well-known there that the establishment's managers were known to keep it open even after closing time if Williams was due in town; they knew he would stop by even if a game ran late. Predictably, the head coach made sure his team's dinner on Thursday night before the Butler game was at Rendezvous.

The Tar Heels were staying at the famous Peabody Hotel, a block down Second Street from Rendezvous. The Peabody, first built in 1869 and then rebuilt in grander form in 1925, is a monument to another era. In both 2009 and 2017, the old gem's lobby turned into a relocated Chapel Hill, with Tar Heel fans from around the country congregating at all hours to meet friends, catch a glimpse of the team, and watch the famous Peabody ducks.

Williams had been an honorary Duckmaster—charged with walking the ducks to and from their top-floor penthouse to their perch in the lobby—in 2009, but he didn't know if he'd have time in 2017. But with grandsons Aiden and Court in town for the games, the proud grandfather eagerly carved out some space in his schedule. Memphis felt like a Williams family trip. At one point, the Hall of Fame head coach could be spotted on the floor of the lobby, wrestling with the grandkids, looking more like a doting granddad than the fiery sideline personality most of the nation might recognize. Not surprisingly, when Williams escorted the ducks back to their top-floor digs, Aiden and Court were right beside him.

North Carolina basketball very rarely gets to be the undercard. But with UCLA and Kentucky playing in the region's second semifinal on Friday night and Butler being the plucky upstart among three of the nation's historic programs, the Tar Heels were as close to being an afterthought as they ever might be. They'd already visited the Civil Rights Museum and heard Rusty Carter's touching first-person account of the era when they'd gone to Memphis in October for a scrimmage. That gave them plenty of time on this visit to walk the ducks and eat some ribs, and Williams wanted to make sure to take advantage. His team was confident but loose.

The trip reunited the Tar Heels with CBS commentator Bill Raftery, who

9
BOUNCING BUTLER

Joel Berry scored a game-high 26 points in the regional semifinal against Butler.
(Photo by J. D. Lyon Jr.)

Coach Williams with his grandsons Court and Aiden during the duck march at the Peabody Hotel in Memphis. (Photo by J. D. Lyon Jr.)

had done the game in Las Vegas against Kentucky. At Carolina's open practice on Thursday afternoon, Raftery was standing on the sideline talking with Williams and Steve Robinson. Pinson saw an opening. He sidled up to the group and put an arm around Raftery.

"If I get a dunk this weekend, could we get a 'Send it in, Theo,' call?" Pinson asked Raftery, referencing the broadcaster's signature call. The group broke up in laughter, but not before Williams got in the last word. "Shoot, Theo," the head coach said, "you haven't had a dunk in two months."

◼ Carolina's annual summer-camp basketball game is supposed to be a fun exhibition. There are two sessions of camp, each one featuring a current-team-against-alumni scrimmage as one of the camp highlights.

It's supposed to be just an easygoing way to entertain the campers, most of whom are already delighted to have spent several nights away from their parents with unlimited access to pizza.

But every player in the game is competitive. And although the first half is often just a dunking exhibition, the second half—first team to 80 wins—gets much more heated, especially as the winning score approaches.

In the summer of 2016, standout Tar Heel point guard Raymond Felton returned to play in the game, as he often does. Felton was a member of the

Justin Jackson scored 24 points, his career high in an NCAA Tourney game, against Butler. (Photo by J. D. Lyon Jr.)

2005 national champions; his teammates and coaches voted him the Most Valuable Player of that team, earning him a spot in the Smith Center rafters. The kid from Latta, South Carolina, had outstanding quickness and was a solid shooter and capable defender, but what set him apart was his intensity. Felton simply hated to lose, which immediately endeared him to Roy Williams when the head coach returned to Carolina from Kansas.

Williams inherited some players who might have been unusual fits with some of his typical recruiting preferences. But as long as Felton was there to channel Williams on the court, the team chemistry could work.

During one of the summer 2016 camp games, several members of the current team were unavailable for a variety of reasons. The alums were thumping the youngsters, and Joel Berry II was taking it poorly. Felton, perhaps recognizing some of himself in the rising junior, took advantage of a dead ball to speak a few quick words to Berry, who was frustrated that his team was shorthanded and that some of his teammates seemed to be giving in to the veterans.

"I know it's the summer," Felton told Berry. "But you have to lead at all times. Be competitive no matter what. To be able to take this team to another level, it starts with you, and you have to be able to get these guys to follow behind you."

"I'm always taking advice from [the Tar Heel alums]," Berry said. "That really changed my perspective."

Felton's words were perfectly directed to Berry, whose fierce competitiveness was never in doubt but whose teammates sometimes perplexed him. Berry held himself to a very high standard and expected the same from his teammates. During his first two seasons at Carolina, he sometimes didn't understand why they couldn't compete the same way he did.

During his freshman season, caught in the rotation behind Marcus Paige, Berry had occasionally been frustrated. He didn't always show it on the court, but he was struggling off the court.

"I got so low that I thought maybe basketball wasn't for me," Berry said. "There were times I went back to my room crying because I love basketball so much, but it was going so badly that it made me almost give up. It was freshman year, and I didn't think I was getting enough playing time. I think I might have shot more air balls in that one year than I had in my whole life of playing basketball. It was hard for me to even see the light of day, because there was so much bad going on. I honestly got to the point that I was either about to decide basketball wasn't for me or to transfer."

Like many freshmen, Berry was convinced the coaches weren't giving him a fair chance. If only they could see it his way, he told friends and family, they would understand why he should be playing more minutes and getting more shots. Almost every freshman in college basketball eventually reaches that point. It's what happens next that determines the course of their college careers.

Unlike many freshmen, though, Berry had well-grounded parents, Joel and Kathie Berry, who didn't have time for his self-pity. At first, they listened and empathized. Eventually, though, they'd had enough.

"They kind of brought me back to life," Berry said. "My parents and I sat down and they told me, 'You know, maybe you need to change your game to show the coaches you should be on the court.' That changed my whole perspective. Sometimes we look at the outside factors rather than at ourselves.

Band director Jeff Fuchs and the Tar Heel pep band offered enthusiastic support throughout the run to the national championship. (Photo by J. D. Lyon Jr.)

Once I looked at myself, I turned my whole game around, and I did what I had to do to be able to show the coaches I deserved to be on the court. That's where my confidence came from, and I started to get that love for basketball again."

That love came in tandem with a fiery on-court personality. Berry demanded much of himself and believed his teammates should do likewise. He hadn't yet developed the ability to recognize that different people have to be pushed in different ways. Williams, a Hall of Fame coach with a lifetime of dealing with people, understood that Isaiah Hicks required a gentler hand, but that Kennedy Meeks could deal with more intense criticism. Berry, a 21-year-old college student, had only one speed. He knew what made him a more effective player and expected everyone else would respond the same way.

So it wasn't out of character for him during the course of the season, when Meeks was frustrated he hadn't received a post entry pass, for Berry to sharply respond, "If you want the ball, then go post up," adding in a couple other adjectives to go with his advice.

Williams immediately pulled Berry aside. "I love your fire," the coach told him. "But you would have been so much more effective saying it to him in another way."

In the last moments before each game, Tar Heel players sit quietly in the locker room awaiting Roy Williams' final pregame thoughts. Behind the head coach on a dry erase board is a list of keys to the game and defensive matchups, a combination of wisdom from Williams and the assistant coach assigned to study that opponent.

Common keys across the six NCAA Tournament games, all scouted by assistants C. B. McGrath and Hubert Davis, emphasized defense, rebounding, and playing at a fast pace while getting good shots, which shouldn't surprise observers familiar with Williams' philosophies.

McGrath's keys to the game against Texas Southern were to run, rebound, and play team defense. The Tar Heels had little difficulty executing the game plan, hitting 51 percent of their shots and ruling the paint with a 54–27 rebounding edge.

Against Arkansas, Davis' keys included boxing out to dominate the offensive glass, limiting turnovers, and defense. Carolina crushed the Razorbacks on the boards and came from behind to win after giving up a big early lead.

"I felt we could get second opportunities by hitting the offensive glass," Davis said. "But we got out to that 17-point lead so quickly, we took our foot off the gas. Arkansas always plays hard the entire game, and it almost cost us the game."

Against Butler, Carolina played so well offensively that McGrath's keys of toughness, rebounding, and quickening the pace almost didn't matter.

"The keys to the game helped our guys' mindsets going into the game," McGrath said. "That was one of our best offensive games of the entire tournament, but we did outrebound them and compete for more loose balls than in some other games."

In the Elite Eight, Davis scouted Kentucky for a second time in three months, helped by firsthand knowledge from the Wildcats' earlier win over Carolina.

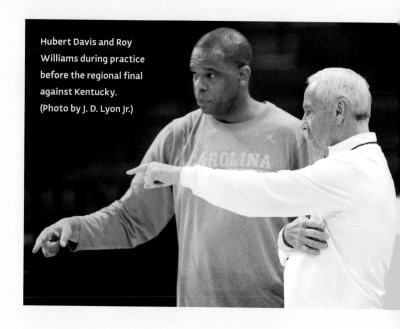

Hubert Davis and Roy Williams during practice before the regional final against Kentucky. (Photo by J. D. Lyon Jr.)

"When we played them earlier, Justin [Jackson] was on Malik Monk twice, and both times Monk didn't get a shot off," said Davis. "I said if we ever play them again, Justin's got to guard Monk. Justin's length and relentlessness did a number on Monk, and he made him play defense on the other end, which tired him out.

"Two individuals changed the entire game for us— Justin and Theo [Pinson]. We put Theo on De'Aaron Fox so Fox would be facing a guy who's just as athletic as he is but a few inches taller. Theo did a great job of keeping Fox in front of him and forced him to shoot when he might've wanted to drive."

Davis drew the scouting assignment for Oregon, citing sharing the ball and offensive spacing as particularly crucial.

"They have the best matchup zone that we've ever played against, so ball movement was going to be important," Davis said. "Their switching and communication were great, just like a man-to-man. Playing Louisville's defense during the season helped us. We didn't mess around with any zone plays, and that's what got us some quality shots."

UNC Players Report
Gonzaga | Apr 3, 2017

Opposing Personnel

	#	Name	YR	HT	WT	PT	RB	Asst/TO	Description	Shot M/Att	3PT M/Att
1	13	Josh Perkins	SO	6-3	190	8.2	2.3	115/72	guard on our own, MUST pressure/contain, contest outside	94-222	60-150
	0	Silas Melson	JR	6-4	195	7.3	2.5	55/30	aggressive on both ends, 3 point shooter, find in transition	94-208	40-105
2	5	Nigel Williams-Goss	JR	6-3	195	16.7	5.9	167/77	great with ball, find early and stay in front, contest every shot, BOX	206-420	40-109
3	4	Jordan Mathews	SR	6-4	203	10.7	3.3	56/30	3 point shooter, make him dribble, find in transition	126-308	79-204
4	3	Johnathan Williams	JR	6-9	228	10.3	6.6	30/50	LH, wants to drive it closer to the goal, RS finisher, strong WALL & BOX	149-251	15-37
	33	Killian Tillie	FR	6-10	200	4.4	3.1	20/20	active/energy guy, WALL & BOX	46-87	11-23
	32	Zach Collins	FR	7-0	230	9.9	5.6	15/54	skilled, make him work for touches and react, strong WALL & BOX	125-191	9-20
5	24	Przemek Karnowski	SR	7-1	300	12.2	5.8	72/64	LH, skilled, make him work for touches, wants to finish RS, strong WALL & BOX	191-318	0-1

Keys to the Game

1 We MUST guard the ball and ball screens the best we ever have!

2 WORK together to get great shots

3 Win the battle on the boards

General Comments

Play hard, play smart & play together! Give everything you have, no regrets!

FINISH THE JOB!!!

Against Gonzaga in the championship game, stifling defense and a persistent offense led to the national title.

"That was the best defense I've seen any team at Carolina play in awhile," McGrath said. "Our bigs were absolutely terrific guarding the ball screens and flattening the ball screens high enough to where Nigel Williams-Goss couldn't attack and go downhill the way he wanted to. They have true big guys who try to score on the block, so they're almost always going to roll to the basket after a screen—they're not going to pop and shoot threes. We knew we'd have time for our big men to get back to their men after they'd slid to stop the ball on ball screens."

After Williams-Goss shot 9 for 16 in Gonzaga's semifinal win over South Carolina, the focused Tar Heel defense and its sliding big men limited the All-America to 5 for 17 shooting. Kennedy Meeks held Bulldog center Przemek Karnowski to nine points on 1 for 9 from the floor.

On the other end, Gonzaga held Carolina to a paltry 4-for-27 effort from three-point range, but the Tar Heels got their good shots inside, dominating points in the paint by a 40–18 margin.

"Offensively, I knew we'd have to work to get great shots because Gonzaga was a very good defensive team, very experienced and good at making you shoot guarded outside jump shots," McGrath said. "We couldn't depend on jump shots to beat them, and we couldn't make any jump shots that night. We just willed it on offense, and it came to our will versus their will. I think our will was more than theirs."

Carolina cheerleaders celebrate the Sweet 16 win in Memphis over Butler. (Photo by J. D. Lyon Jr.)

Berry is a smart player who is also a basketball sponge. He'd always assumed that getting the best out of his teammates meant giving them the ball at the right time or making a shot himself to help them beat a rival. But Williams' advice introduced a relatively new idea: understanding his teammates' personalities, and perhaps adapting his own accordingly, might have tangible benefits on the court. This was an aspect of the game that Berry's roommate, Theo Pinson, understood intuitively. Berry, who loves anything that makes him a better basketball player, was fascinated.

Williams was an important resource as Berry tried to develop leadership skills, as were other older Tar Heels.

"I was saying the right thing," Berry said, "but I was saying it the wrong way. Coach helped me so much, and so did Marcus Paige. When he got here, he didn't talk as much. But to be a point guard here, you have to be vocal, and you have to lead by example. By his senior year, whether things were going wrong or going well, you always heard Marcus talking. I tried to follow that example.

"I've made progress, because I love challenges. So I tried to be more of a vocal leader, and I was able to reach that point, but I wasn't being vocal in the

way Coach wanted me to be. So then I became a better vocal leader. By the end of this season, I felt myself saying things differently than I would have as a freshman or a sophomore. I think my teammates saw that I was trying to use my fire on the court and not toward them, and they respected that. I tried to show them I have respect for them as a person, and that's why I had to change the way I was saying things."

Even in Berry's more-enlightened state, there was still one person who never received any breaks: himself. He'd learned how to manage his teammates more effectively, but the last hurdle was ensuring he didn't redline his own emotions during a game.

Already, as a junior, he'd allowed his emotions to render him ineffective in the loss at Miami. Foul trouble took him out of the Duke game in Brooklyn, but his own frustration kept him on the bench; Berry likely would have returned to the game sooner if he hadn't looked so disheartened.

Williams and his point guard had repeated conversations about the best way to manage his emotions. They were tested again against Butler in the round of 16, as Bulldogs guard Kamar Baldwin tried to play physically against Berry. Twice, the Bulldogs made hard contact with Berry after the whistle blew.

In some ways, the Bulldogs' chippy play was exactly what Carolina needed. Berry didn't have time to think about his still-gimpy ankle or the shooting slump that had left him without a two-point field goal in the Tar Heels' first two NCAA Tournament games. Suitably challenged, he responded in exactly the way Williams wanted. First, he drove to the rim and scored through contact. Then he used a stutter step to get another hoop.

"When guys try to talk junk to Joel during a game, I always tell them, 'You just messed up. You should never do that,'" said Pinson. "It's just the type of guy he is. He's already mad, and you're just going to make him even more mad."

Berry finished with 26 points, and Justin Jackson added 24, combining for 50 of Carolina's 92 points in the 12-point win. The third source of offense was a little more unexpected.

Luke Maye did not make a three-point shot in Greenville and contributed just three rebounds against Arkansas. His usually reliable perimeter shot was faltering, and he airballed a trifecta against the Hogs.

During the Tar Heels' three days at home between Greenville and Memphis, Maye stopped by Hubert Davis' office. At the time, he was 2-for-9 from the three-point line in his last eight games.

"I don't know what's going on," Maye said to Davis. "I haven't been shooting well at all."

Davis, a basketball lifer, admired Maye for taking the initiative to come talk to him. He understood the courage it took to step into a coach's office

When guys try to talk junk to Joel during a game, I always tell them, "You just messed up. You should never do that." He's already mad, and you're just going to make him even more mad.

—THEO PINSON

and admit uncertainty, and he also recognized the intelligence it required to admit something wasn't quite right.

"Right now, Luke, there's a difference between the Luke who plays with the blue team in practice and the Luke who plays with the white team in games," Davis told him. "In games, you're trying to please the coach. You should always listen to the coach, but you should never try to please the coach. When we scout an opponent, the hardest thing for us to guard is a stretch four. You have that ability, and it wreaks havoc on a defense. I would hate to play against you. There's a reason Coach recruited you. Don't be afraid to be that player."

The confidence boost was exactly what Maye needed. In practice, he had no hesitation and was willing to fire whenever he saw an opening. In games, however, he sometimes deferred to the players he saw as bigger stars. Sure, he could take this shot, but what if Jackson had a better window? That tiny hesitation was enough to throw off his shot.

"Justin and Joel are our number one and number two," Maye said. "So when I'm playing with them, it's harder for me to know when I should shoot. Going into Memphis, I decided I was going to shoot it no matter what happened."

Maye made six of his ten field-goal attempts and three of his five three-pointers against Butler. His 16 points and 12 rebounds gave him his first career double-double. He was in such a groove that Williams altered the usual Tar Heel rotation, leaving Maye on the floor for a career-high-tying 25 minutes.

The sophomore was so hot that when Williams called his use-it-or-lose-it timeout in the first half—even the notoriously timeout-averse head coach took a slightly different approach in the NCAA Tournament—the Tar Heels came out of the break and ran a play for Maye, not the typical set for Berry or Jackson.

"When Coach left me in, I felt like if he believed in me to play me, then I needed to keep on playing my game," Maye said. "I had usually been in for three or four minutes rather than long stretches, and that really gets you in the flow."

Maye was in such a good rhythm that he was summoned to the postgame press conference, normally the domain of the team's biggest stars. After meeting with the media, Maye, Berry, and Jackson headed back to the Tar Heel locker room.

"Hey, there goes the Big Three," said an onlooker. The comment was slightly tongue-in-cheek, but on this night, it was true.

"I really embraced that comment," Maye said. "I took it into the Kentucky game, and I felt like I went into that game with the most confidence I'd had all year."

Joel Berry and Justin Jackson combined for 50 points against Butler.
(Photo by Robert Crawford)

Cultivating Luke Maye's confidence had been an ongoing process throughout the season. Earlier in the year, as Maye struggled during some of the nonconference schedule, Roy Williams found the sophomore in the basketball office late one night after a game. Maye was finishing a paper that was due the next day, while Williams was preparing for the next day's practice.

Somewhat unexpectedly, the duo began a conversation about Maye's role and his practice performance as compared to his game performance. At the time, Justin Jackson was exploding into a National Player-of-the-Year candidate, Joel Berry II was playing at an elite level, and the Tar Heels were generally recognized nationally as one of the best teams in the country. Life was good. But Williams felt Maye would be an important cog as the season progressed and wanted to cultivate his development.

"He talked a lot with me about moving on to the next play," Maye said. "He told me how he feels that if I start well, I finish well, but if I struggle early, it gets tougher for me throughout the game. Toward the end of the year, I got better about keeping my head high whether I made a good play or a bad play. I grew as a player in that area, and that talk with Coach gave me a lot of confidence. He told me if I played my game and played my strengths, I could be a great player at Carolina. It really showed me how much trust he had in my game."

Despite Maye's double-double against Butler, very few observers were talking about him as the Tar Heels prepared to play Kentucky for the right to go to the Final Four. Given the first meeting of the year and the pedigrees of the two programs, this was the marquee game of the tournament so far.

NCAA rules required the players and Williams to spend over an hour fulfilling various media obligations on Saturday, the day before the game. Unfailingly, the media wanted to know how the Tar Heels planned to defend sensational Kentucky freshman Malik Monk, who had scored 47 points against Carolina in Las Vegas.

The Tar Heels certainly hadn't forgotten about Monk. Hubert Davis researched the single-game scoring production of every Division I player in the country during the 2016–17 season. He found that only four players in America had scored more in a single game than Monk's 47 during the year, and none of those four were from Power Five conferences. Davis peppered the scouting report with references to Monk's 47 points.

"I want to tell you guys something," Davis said to the team during their scouting meeting. "Monk scored 47 points, and he had zero rebounds, zero fouls, and zero assists. You know what that means? He scored 47 points, and he rested anytime he wasn't shooting. He wasn't worried about defending anybody. You have to be kidding me. He didn't respect anyone else on this team enough to even guard anybody. He felt like he could rest against any one of you guys."

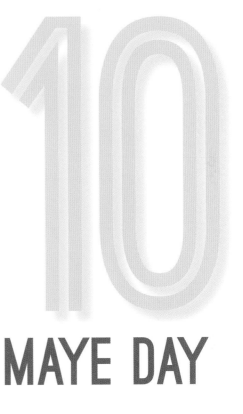

10
MAYE DAY

Kennedy Meeks pulled down a career-high 17 rebounds against Kentucky.

(Photo by Jim Hawkins)

Stilman White's reverse layup was a key basket in the Kentucky game after Joel Berry was sidelined with an injury. (Photo by Kevin Cox/Getty Images)

Williams gave his team a similarly pointed message.

"I wanted them to understand we could not give Kentucky the open shots we did in Vegas," he said. "We were awful defensively in Vegas. Monk had time to check the wind gauge before he shot every dadgum shot. Bam (Adebayo) dominated our big guys. (De'Aaron) Fox dominated our guards.

"We couldn't think that we could go out there and go through the motions in practice. They had to get more out of the scouting report. They had to get more out of practice. We emphasized this was not a typical scouting report. This was the scouting report to go to the Final Four."

Justin Jackson defended Malik Monk and was surprisingly vocal during UNC's win over the Wildcats. (Photo by J. D. Lyon Jr.)

Everyone assumed that the Kentucky scouting report would include giving Theo Pinson the assignment to defend Monk. Pinson was unavailable in the first game, and it seemed the natural fit to put the player publicly acknowledged as Carolina's best defender (an opinion the coaches did not always share) on the opponent's most-explosive offensive player.

Williams and his coaching staff had another idea. Pinson's best defensive skill was guarding the ball and using his height to combat ballhandlers. Justin Jackson's best defensive skill, meanwhile, was getting around screens and allowing his wingspan to distract shooters.

So why, then, would they put Pinson on Monk, who scored most of his points off screens? Fox had been terrific against UCLA, and completely focusing on Monk would probably allow Fox to have a sensational game. So why not put Pinson on Fox and Jackson on Monk?

"I had guarded point guards recently, and I guarded [NC State's] Cat Barber last year," Pinson said. "Justin put more length on Monk, and since Monk explodes really high on his jumper, Justin would affect him a little more. I'm more comfortable guarding point guards who are speedy and can get to the rim. We tried to throw something different at them that they weren't mentally prepared for."

No one outside the Carolina locker room seemed prepared for it. At Saturday's media session, Williams received multiple questions about Pinson's chances of stopping Monk. With Pinson sitting beside him grinning, Williams played along.

During NCAA Tournament play, teams are required to have one open practice before the first game of a weekend. So Carolina practiced in front of the FedExForum crowd on Thursday, prior to the game against Butler. But practices before the regional championship games are closed.

So when the players and coaches met the media late on Saturday afternoon, they didn't mention that the Tar Heels had just left a 90-minute practice during which they'd worked on Jackson guarding Monk and Pinson defending Fox. Of course, they also didn't mention that during the course of that practice, Berry had injured his ankle again.

This time, it was during a zone defense drill, which was even more frustrating to Williams, since he is a devoted fan of man-to-man defense. But as Steve Robinson had suggested before the tournament, zone would almost certainly be needed eventually, so the Tar Heels devoted a quick practice period to reviewing their zone.

During that session, Berry stepped on Kennedy Meeks' foot. The injury was painful enough that Berry left the court. Berry went into the locker room with athletics trainer Doug Halverson. Williams initially stayed on the court, then went to the locker room, where he found a very frustrated point guard.

"Relax," the head coach told him. "Getting mad isn't going to help us. Just relax and let Doug take a look at it."

Williams went back to the court, and when Halverson emerged from the locker room, he told the coach, "Joel's in a better place now." Berry rejoined his team, and Williams allowed him to go through a handful of possessions, just to build his confidence that he could play on the injury. "That's all we needed to see," Williams said as Berry ran down the court. "You can do this."

"I was trying to encourage him," Williams said. "He was getting tougher with every weekend, and we had to have him do it again."

That evening, the Tar Heels gathered for their normal late-night snack in a Peabody Hotel meeting room. They went over the scouting report again—Pinson was still designated to guard Fox, with Jackson on Monk—and reviewed the offensive and defensive keys.

As Meeks looked around the room, the reality that this could be the last time the 2017 Tar Heels would be together began to hit him. He saw Nate Britt, who had become like a brother. He saw Hicks, his roommate for four years. He saw Williams, who had pushed and prodded and pleaded with him for four years.

Luke Maye scored a career-high 17 points, including this three-pointer that gave UNC a 50–45 lead, in the 75–73 win over Kentucky. (Photo by J. D. Lyon Jr.)

Meeks decided he had to speak.

"In the Butler game, I didn't feel like I was there for my team," he said. "I felt like I kind of let them down. I wanted to put all the years I had messed up on the defensive end, or gotten an attitude with Coach, behind me. As the film session went on, I just had a feeling we could do something great, and I had to stand up and say something.

"I'm an emotional person. So I was already tearing up a little bit. I told the guys that no matter what happens, we had to play our hardest, and we had to dominate. I told them all that matters at the end of the day is what Coach says. I reminded them of how we felt last year after Villanova, when we got

so close. And I do think that added a little fire to being able to play Kentucky. At that point, it didn't really matter who stepped up. All that mattered was us finding a way to win."

Just like in Las Vegas, Kentucky traveled with thousands of fans. But plenty of Tar Heels made the trip, also, and Wildcats coach John Calipari had a long and complicated history with the city of Memphis that led some locals to support Carolina. The FedExForum crowd was pro-Kentucky, but not as overwhelmingly as might have been expected in an SEC town, and certainly not as significantly as the crowd in Birmingham had been when Carolina beat Kentucky in the 1995 NCAA Tournament in similar circumstances.

When the game began, Williams' defensive adjustments immediately paid dividends. Monk made just one of his first four field goals, but even more importantly, he was able to hoist just five shots in the entire first half. He showed some visible frustration midway through the first half when some contact away from the ball left him on the floor, leaving him glaring at the official while play continued around him. Later in the possession, he forced and missed a jumper.

"Justin had asked if he could guard some of the best players we faced in the postseason," Williams said. "He had the confidence and wanted the challenge. Down the stretch, he wanted to guard the other team's best scorer. He was excited about guarding Malik. He developed so much that he went from being a liability defensively to being at the level that he wanted the challenge. He asked to guard Malik because he knew he was capable of doing it."

The defensive surge energized Jackson, who was visibly enjoying the challenge. His 11 first-half points were a game high and almost double Monk's six. After Jackson turned an offensive rebound into a layup to give Carolina a nine-point lead, he returned some of the chirping Monk had been providing on the other end.

"Malik had blocked Joel's shot on a fast break, and he said something to Joel," Jackson said. "I got the rebound and laid it back in, so I said something back to him. He tried to start jawing, and he just kept talking. Joel kind of joined in when we got to half-court. It kept escalating. You can kind of get caught up in the moment. But, for me, I didn't want him to be disrespectful to my teammate. I was kind of taking up for Joel, but it was also a heat-of-the-moment type thing."

It was a slightly unexpected side of the usually quiet Jackson. But this was the regional final against Kentucky, and even with all the talent on the court, Jackson looked extremely comfortable in his role as an alpha player in the season's biggest game. He defended, he scored, and he even jawed a little when needed.

"I saw him doing it one time during the game," Williams said. "I didn't say anything to him, because it was working. It was not typical of Justin. But I thought it was because he knew he was playing well defensively and he was enjoying that part of it. It was the enthusiasm of being successful on the defensive end of the floor."

Meanwhile, the other half of the defensive switch was also paying dividends, but partially for unexpected reasons. Due to foul trouble, Fox was limited to just eight minutes in a first half that Carolina led, 38–33, and Pinson had done a credible job defending him. But two of Fox's fouls had come via the hustle of reserve point guard Stilman White, who drew two quick fouls during a three-minute stretch and also sank a big reverse layup at a time Carolina was struggling.

"Sometimes you have to fake it to make it," White said. "It's a mindset. I wanted to be confident and aggressive and show I belonged out there."

It was fitting that a reserve would make big plays in the first half, because it set the stage for perhaps the biggest NCAA Tournament contribution ever from a Tar Heel substitute. With Carolina holding a 45–41 lead with 14 minutes remaining, Maye scored eight straight points.

First, he converted a left-handed layup. Then, he pump-faked to lose defender Derek Willis, took one dribble, and nailed a three-pointer in a perfect echo of the thousands of shooting drills he'd done with Jackson over the summer. Then he flashed to the post, received a gorgeous pass from Pinson, and scored through contact from Willis. By the time he swished the free

UNC overcame a five-point deficit with less than five minutes to play to beat No. 2 seed Kentucky. (Photo by J. D. Lyon Jr.)

throw after a media timeout, he'd scored six points in 49 seconds and eight in the last 3:02, and Carolina led 53–47.

Kentucky surged to a five-point lead behind some unexpected scoring from Isaac Humphries, but then Carolina used a timely switch to the same zone defense the coaches had pondered on Selection Sunday to spark a 12–0 run—including 6-for-6 from the free-throw line for Pinson and Maye. The spurt enabled Carolina to take a seven-point lead with 54 seconds remaining.

Seven points in less than a minute? That should be enough, right? But after being bottled up for 39 minutes of the game, Fox and Monk suddenly exploded, combining to hit three three-pointers between them, the last one an improbable Monk jumper with Jackson and Maye draped over him that tied the score with 7.2 seconds remaining.

The Kentucky comeback had happened so quickly that there wasn't even time to develop that sense of foreboding that usually accompanies a shriveling lead. Just a week ago, the Tar Heels had made their largest-ever NCAA Tournament comeback; this one from the Wildcats had been two more points in two fewer minutes. It was stunning.

Except that the Tar Heels weren't stunned.

What happened over the next 7.2 seconds had been drilled into them over the previous 95 practices. Meeks grabbed the ball out of the net and quickly took a hop behind the baseline so he could inbound the ball. Later, Calipari would lament not being able to stop play and set his defense.

Carolina's win over Kentucky was UNC's 20th in 27 regional finals. (Photo by J. D. Lyon Jr.)

Championships are often remembered for a winning or iconic shot in the title game. One needs to look no further than Michael Jordan's jumper "from out on the left" to beat Georgetown in 1982. That is, undoubtedly, the most famous shot in Carolina Basketball history and one of the truly indelible images in sports, a shot that launched the career of the transformative player ESPN called the Greatest Athlete of the 20th Century.

Joel Berry II's three-pointer to reclaim the lead over Gonzaga and Isaiah Hicks' bucket with 26 seconds to play are two of the most important baskets in the 2017 NCAA title game, but the shot that defined the 2017 season is Luke Maye's 19-footer with 0.3 seconds left to beat Kentucky in the South Region final.

Maye, a sophomore from Huntersville, North Carolina, came into the Sweet 16 averaging 5.8 points in less than 14 minutes per game, but he had 16 points and a dozen rebounds against Butler and netted a career-high 17 against Kentucky. He forever cemented his place in Carolina Basketball history with his winning shot against the Wildcats, the No. 2 seed loaded with NBA lottery picks.

"Being a kid from a small town outside Charlotte and always dreaming of playing at this university and having a role on a national championship team, to be put in that group with some of the best shots in Carolina history is really a spectacular feeling," said the soft-spoken Maye.

His shot didn't win the national championship like Jordan's did, but it sent the Tar Heels to the Final Four. UNC has now won the NCAA Tournament six times. In some of those years, there are signature shots like Jordan's or Maye's, but in others a more collective body of work stood out the most.

Pete Brennan's jump shot late in the first overtime in the 1957 semifinals against Michigan State and Joe Quigg's go-ahead free throws with six seconds to play in the third overtime the following night against

Luke Maye's reaction after sending Carolina to the Final Four with a jump shot with 0.3 seconds to play. (Photo by Andy Lyons/Getty Images)

The shot that made Luke Maye a Tar Heel hero forever and the South Regional Most Outstanding Player. (Photo by Justin Ford/ USA Today Sports Images)

Kansas are readily identified as the key plays in UNC winning its first NCAA title.

Jordan's jumper against Georgetown and James Worthy's spectacular dunk over fellow Gastonia native Sleepy Floyd in '82 are images as fresh today as they were 35 years ago. The championship game in 1993 is best remembered for a series of three-pointers by Donald Williams and the infamous timeout/technical foul by Michigan's Chris Webber. The most famous basket that season arguably came in January, when

George Lynch stole a cross-court pass and raced in for a dunk to put the Tar Heels ahead and erase Florida State's 21-point lead in one of Carolina's greatest comeback wins.

Likewise in 2005, Sean May's six games of brilliance, Raymond Felton's late three-pointer against Illinois in the championship game, and Marvin Williams' go-ahead tip-in in that same game stand out, but Williams' three-point play to beat Duke in the final regular-season game was the play of the year. Many observers say they've never heard the Smith Center louder than when Williams capped a 10–0 run to give UNC the lead with seconds to play.

Four years later, the Tar Heels won by an average of 20.2 points per game in the NCAA Tournament and led every minute in the second half in the last four contests. Carolina put on a clinic in the first half of the championship against the Spartans, including a three-point bomb by Wayne Ellington that was part of his 17-point first half and helped him win Final Four MVP honors.

Maye's shot makes any list of greatest Tar Heel moments, not only because it sent UNC to Phoenix where the Tar Heels cut down the nets, but also because it had a "you've got to be kidding me" Hollywood storyline.

Maye came to Carolina as a walk-on, earned a scholarship as a freshman, and is the son of a former Tar Heel quarterback. He scored in double figures as many times in the 2017 NCAA Tournament (3) as he did in his first 64 games as a Tar Heel. When Theo Pinson raced upcourt with the game tied at 73, most thought he would drive to the basket or dish the ball to ACC Player of the Year Justin Jackson, who was open on the wing in front of Carolina's bench.

Instead, Pinson slid the ball to Maye, and not one Tar Heel coach or player doubted what the outcome would be.

"Theo had the ball top of the key center line, and in my mind, I'm saying, 'Make a play, make a play,'" said Roy Williams. "He penetrated and threw it to Luke. Before [Luke] let it go, I thought it was going in. Everything felt right, the tempo felt right, Kentucky wasn't picked up. Luke drills our starters in practice five days out of six, so Theo making that pass was as good a play as he could possibly do."

Indeed, Kennedy Meeks getting the ball in play before Kentucky could call timeout, Pinson's aggressive but heady ballhandling, and Maye sprinting downcourt and sinking a shot he'd practiced thousands of times—but never with as much on the line as a trip to the Final Four—all add up to a play that will certainly stand the test of time and be remembered as the play of the year for the 2017 national champions.

"I probably should've called a timeout," the Kentucky coach said. "But they got that ball in so quick, I couldn't get anybody to do it. But I needed to stop that right there."

It wasn't by accident.

"Coach always says to get the ball out quick," Meeks said. "My main objective was to get it out quick and give it to somebody who can push the ball up the court pretty fast. Everything that Coach says comes into play eventually, and you run into a situation where something he says is going to matter and dictate the end of the game. You sit in practice and wonder why we're doing this and think, 'What's the point?' Then you're put in a position in a game where it saves your season. It was so much of a habit for me to get it out quickly, because I was trained to do that. At that moment in time, it was essential for us."

On the quick inbounds, Adebayo overplayed Berry slightly. That left Meeks staring at Pinson, who was all alone on the right side of the court, just in front of a wildly celebrating Kentucky bench.

The junior turned and sprinted up court. Some of Williams' lessons were playing in his head.

"I looked up at the clock, and I saw seven seconds," Pinson said. "Coach usually tells us if the clock is under seven, call a timeout. I looked over at Joel, and someone was guarding the ball in my line of sight. I thought, 'Just get downhill as fast as you can.' Adebayo was behind me, so I wanted to attack, because everything was one-on-one. It looked like their defensive balance was not good. Of course they're still reacting to Monk making a great shot, so the first thing that went through my mind when I got the ball was, 'Go, go, go.' Attack. Make a play."

As he crossed midcourt, Pinson had ACC Player of the Year Justin Jackson on the right wing in front of the Tar Heel bench. He also had Maye running hard down the court a half-step in front of Willis. Maye thought perhaps he had a lane to the rim and raised his hand for a pass. Pinson saw him.

"I thought he might pitch it ahead to me," Maye said. "But Theo had that look in his eye that he usually gets when he's trying to get to the basket."

There was perhaps a very tiny window through which Pinson could have tried to squeeze the ball to Maye. The freshman version of Pinson, prone to attempt the spectacular play, might have tried to make the pass. The more-seasoned version of Pinson, however, knew better. "I saw his hand go up," he said. "But I wasn't going to throw it to him then. Once I got across half-court, I wanted Willis to either commit to me and Luke was going to have a shot, or I was going to get a layup."

Pinson took two more dribbles to force Willis to make a decision. Fox stayed in front of him and essentially screened off Willis, moving him back

> It felt good when it came off my hand. When it went in, that's the best feeling I've ever had in the history of my sports career.
>
> —LUKE MAYE

Coach Williams got soaked in a very happy
Carolina locker room following the win that sent
the Tar Heels to Phoenix for the Final Four.
(Photo by J. D. Lyon Jr.)

toward the rim. With three players moving under the basket, that left Maye
standing almost alone 18 feet from the hoop.

Jackson and Berry, of course, drew major defensive attention. Pinson
flared just a step to his left to clear a little more space on Maye's side of the
court, then dropped the ball to the sophomore. When Maye caught it, there
were 2.7 seconds remaining on the clock.

"He's going to make that," Pinson thought to himself. "He shoots that all
the time."

Berry, trailing the play near the top of the key, had a similar thought.

"Luke stepped into it," he said. "And when I saw him take his time and follow through, I thought, 'I think that's good.'"

(Photo by J. D. Lyon Jr.)

Luke Maye

My family actually told me they left right after the game. They walked out, because they thought we would leave right away. So they had to talk their way back into the arena.

When I look at this picture, I see people who really care a lot about me and about what we stand for as a family. To have all of us there together for a game like this was such a great feeling. I'm so blessed to be able to enjoy that experience with them and to have people like this in my life.

Luke Maye addresses the media after
UNC beat Kentucky in the South Region final.
(Photo by Joe Murphy/NCAA Photos)

Therein was the difference between the rest of the world and the players on the team, who watched Maye every day in practice. As a freshman, he had been the source of much frustration for Marcus Paige. With Paige on the white (starters) team and Maye on the blue (reserves) team, Maye made a habit of scorching the white squad, usually leading to some extra running.

"Luke has hit so many shots over me in practice," Hicks said. "So, so many. Last year, there were times at practice where Marcus would get really mad at Brice and me, because we couldn't guard Luke, and the blue team was killing us."

All those shooting drills with Jackson over the summer. All those conversations with Williams and Davis. All the game minutes building his confidence. Everything led to those 7.2 seconds and that one shot, when Luke Maye was the most important player on a court filled with future NBA Draft picks.

Maye's shot swished through, barely even touching the rim, sending the arena into pandemonium. Carolina led 75–73, and only 0.3 seconds remained.

"It felt good when it came off my hand," Maye said. "When it went in, that's the best feeling I've ever had in the history of my sports career."

It was the most improbable ending to a regional final in Carolina Basketball history. Cheers of "Luuuuuuuuuuuuke" echoed through the FedExForum.

In the aftermath, on a court filled with hugs and smiles and can-you-believe-it laughter, Berry hobbled down the ladder after cutting his piece of net, gingerly trying to determine how to walk down a ladder with one good leg. Eventually, Pinson stepped forward and helped him take the last couple of steps.

Williams traditionally takes the last snip of the net, so as his players took turns passing off the scissors, the head coach was back near midcourt, standing alone. In the frenzy of a postgame celebration, it's very rare for the head coach to get any time to himself. There are media responsibilities, administrators who want to offer congratulations, and dozens of handshakes.

For about 30 seconds, however, Williams was completely on his own. He watched as his players laughed and celebrated. Tears welled in his eyes.

"I was thinking about last year, and about Georgia Tech, and Theo and all the tough things we had gone through," Williams said. "I always say one of the best things about coaching is seeing the looks on your players' faces when they accomplish something that is really hard to do. I've always said that I would like to just sit over on the bench and watch my team celebrate when they win a big game, but I can never do it, because there are so many things to do. But in that moment, I was able to think about all those things and watch them, and it was a moment that I treasured."

The Tar Heels boarded the plane in Memphis and arrived back home after

Carolina's seniors celebrated with the
South Region championship hardware.
(Photo by Robert Crawford)

midnight. Most had class the next day, including Maye, who had already received a reminder from a very important person.

"My mom called me when [my parents] were on the way home from Memphis and said, 'Luke, don't forget to go to your business class, because you'll get behind if you don't go,'" Maye said with a smile. "We got back around 1:00 A.M. To be honest, I really wasn't feeling it, but I made a promise to my mom that I would do well in school."

As would soon make the rounds of social media, Maye was greeted with a standing ovation by his classmates in his 8:00 A.M. business class, taught by professor C. J. Skender. Maye, who hates individual attention, gave an awkward wave to his classmates.

"My mom and dad tell me all the time how important school is and what it means to the rest of your life," he said. "Basketball is such a big part of this university, and those people in that class are my peers. To get a standing ovation from them was incredible."

On the day after Carolina's epic win over Kentucky, Roy Williams sent his staff home for lunch. Luke Maye's shot was less than 24 hours old. The UNC campus was still in a state of celebratory giddiness. And Williams wanted his staff to take a break.

It was a tiny detail, but it was indicative of the program Williams tries to run. Families of staff members were invited to travel with the team throughout the postseason. Assistant coach Hubert Davis' kids were old enough to have their own activities; it wasn't unusual for Williams to change a practice time so Davis could watch his oldest son, Elijah, play in an eighth-grade basketball game. If the time couldn't be changed, Williams would nudge Davis midway through practice and tell him it was time to leave. Elijah's game was more important than another Tar Heel practice.

Williams' priorities came from his own experiences as a coach with a young family. When his children, Scott and Kimberly, were growing up, Williams tried to be involved with them as frequently as possible. But he felt he'd missed some opportunities.

"Coach told me one time he felt like the one mistake he made as a coach was missing a lot of Scott's games," Davis said. "He said he didn't know why he missed them; he was the head coach and could change practice however he wanted. He told me he didn't want any of his coaches to have that same regret."

And so Micah Davis serves as a Tar Heel ballboy, and Elijah Davis sits on the bench with the team during games, just as Denzel Robinson—Steve's son—did when he was Elijah's age. And even after a pulsating win to earn a spot in the Final Four, Williams sent his coaches home for lunch.

With only a week left in the season, with Carolina one of just four remaining teams with an opportunity to win the national title, Williams was running a program instead of just coaching a team. Would staying at the office and reviewing 30 more minutes of film really make a difference in Saturday's game against Oregon? Probably not. Williams knew his coaches well enough to know they would eventually watch that film, anyway.

It had been an extraordinarily long season, with dozens of nights away and thousands of air miles. On this day, for this hour, the head coach wanted his staff to remember exactly what was most important in their lives.

The perspective translated to his team. After their arrival in Phoenix, the Tar Heels went through a somewhat grim practice. Steve Robinson didn't like the tone of the session.

"We weren't worried about having fun or taking it all in," said Nate Britt. "We felt like we had done that last year. So we wanted to beat Oregon and then beat whoever we played next."

It wasn't the mood the coaches wanted to set. All season long, they'd talked about the fun the 2016 team had enjoyed while making it to the Final

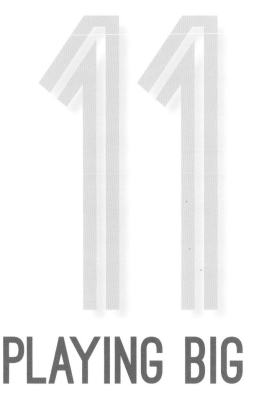

11
PLAYING BIG

Joel Berry played around in CBS's green screen room two days before the national semifinals. (Photo by J. D. Lyon Jr.)

139

Carolina held a closed practice at the stadium on Thursday of Final Four week. (Photo by J. D. Lyon Jr.)

Four. Now that the 2017 team had earned a trip to Phoenix, they'd lost some of that joy.

"You guys need to realize that you've gone to back-to-back Final Fours," Robinson told the team during practice. "This doesn't happen. Teams don't do this. You need to have fun and enjoy it."

Theo Pinson expressed a similar viewpoint when he talked to his teammates. "I wanted to bring back the point of last year," he said. "The thing that drove us last year was that we were having so much fun, and we enjoyed the journey so much. That drove us not to lose, because we wanted to do anything it took not to lose so we could keep having fun with each other in all these different venues. I wanted us to remember this year to do everything we could so we could keep this train moving."

With an extra day in Phoenix because of travel concerns about Joel Berry II's ankle, the Tar Heels had some extra opportunities to spend time together. Pinson, Berry, Brandon Robinson, and Shea Rush spent hours at the Final Four FanFest, enjoying the interactive games. Most players attended a

Joel Berry and Theo Pinson at FanFest. (Photo by J. D. Lyon Jr.)

Brandon Robinson and Kenny Williams showed off their passing skills at FanFest. (Photo by J. D. Lyon Jr.)

Coach Williams, Justin Jackson, and Theo Pinson at the pre–Final Four press conference. (Photo by J. D. Lyon Jr.)

Phoenix Suns game. Recovery workouts took place in the rooftop hotel pool; on one side of the deck, Jonas Sahratian and Doug Halverson worked out players in the pool, while on the other side, fans celebrated Carolina's Final Four appearance in a hotel restaurant.

Meeks joined his teammates at the pool on Thursday night, 48 hours before the game against Oregon. Quietly, he'd grabbed a mammoth 17 rebounds against Kentucky. He'd posted double-figure rebounds in every NCAA Tournament game except the opener against Texas Southern, when he was needed for just 17 minutes. Most of his large and supportive family—Williams was known to joke that his in-home visit with Meeks was the only one he'd ever seen in which 18 family members attended—was in Phoenix for the games.

It was a potentially storybook way for the Charlotte native to end a career that had not always been smooth. Meeks had well-chronicled weight issues upon his arrival at Carolina. Williams describes losing weight as, "according to people who know, one of the hardest things in the world," and Meeks put in the work to fulfill Williams' lose-weight-or-you-don't-play ultimatum.

But Meeks was also known to frustrate the coaches with occasional lapses in judgment or effort. He almost always said the right thing, but early in his career, his actions didn't always follow his words. As even Meeks would admit, his family sometimes coddled him. It was a new experience for him to have an adult constantly barking at him and expecting more. The dynamic created a sometimes-unpredictable relationship in which Williams would often be the bad cop and Davis the good cop.

It wasn't unusual for Williams to blast Meeks at practice and the big man to seek out Davis afterward.

"I told him so many times that when he should really be worried is when Coach stopped talking to him," Davis said. "As long as your coach is talking to you, that means he cares about you. He sees something in you that you don't see. I wouldn't say that Kennedy ever got to the point that he liked Coach getting on him. But he did get to the point that he understood that he needed it."

In true Meeks fashion, even after the season, he wasn't completely willing to admit that Williams had always been correct. But he did begin to understand how to learn from his coach even when he didn't agree with him.

"I think we wound up developing a mutual respect for each other," Meeks said. "He's the greatest coach I've ever had. Anything he throws at us, it's because he wants to make us a tougher, better team. We didn't always see eye to eye as much as he did with other players, but I learned so much about how to become a man and how to respect everybody."

As a senior, Meeks began making some subtle changes in his work habits. A handful of players worked out before and after every practice, refining certain skills. Meeks was usually among that group. The change in his body was undeniable. And when his senior year arrived, Meeks suddenly realized it was his last opportunity.

"Everything with Coach prepared me for anything that came at me," Meeks said. "I tried to do everything I could so I would know at the end of the day that I had tried my hardest and left everything on the court. All those years of losing games we shouldn't have lost, I put all of that behind me."

It doesn't mean Meeks was perfect throughout the year. After one Carolina loss, the Tar Heels went through their normal film session the next day. Following a defeat, those hours are usually filled with winding and rewinding the film to highlight mistakes. Then Williams asks the assistant coaches if they have anything to add.

Usually, Davis declines to speak. This time, though, he spoke up.

"I was talking to everybody, but really I was talking to Kennedy," he said.

"When are you going to change?" Davis asked the room. "We've watched the film over and over and seen the same mistakes every time. At some point, you're going to have to change. My second year in the NBA, I was with the Knicks, and I didn't play in two games of the NBA Finals. The reason is because Pat Riley couldn't trust me defensively. At that point, I decided I was going to change who I was on the defensive end. I got into the best shape of my life. I watched film. I looked at the scouting reports. As bad as I was

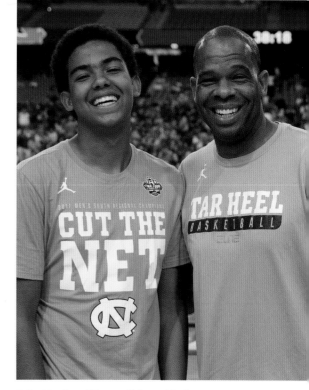

Hubert Davis and his son Elijah at Friday's open practice at University of Phoenix Stadium. (Photo by J. D. Lyon Jr.)

Coach Williams and Brandon Robinson at the
Final Four. (Photo by J. D. Lyon Jr.)

defensively, if I was capable of making that change, then all of you could do it, too."

Meeks understood the message. He won the team's defensive player of the game award three times in his first 131 career games as a Tar Heel. But he won it six of the final 13 games of his career, including NCAA Tournament contests against Arkansas, Kentucky, and Gonzaga. His 17 rebounds against an athletic, talented Wildcats team in the regional final were a sign of his progress. Always emotional, Meeks—more than any other senior— understood his time as a Carolina basketball player was close to an end. He was determined to play two more games as a Tar Heel, and to make them memorable.

■ The Final Four was practically an annual holiday for Williams. One of his favorite days of the season is open-practice day when his team is a Final Four participant, as he loves the opportunity to be on the court with his team in front of the entire basketball world. Since April 1 was Elijah Davis' birthday, Williams invited Hubert Davis' oldest son on the team bus to the arena and in the locker room before the practice.

That evening, he used the team bus to take a couple dozen friends and family to dinner. In true Williams fashion, he was worried that his use of the bus might not be appropriate. "Are you sure it's OK to use the team bus?" he asked senior associate athletic director Clint Gwaltney, the athletic department liaison for men's basketball. Gwaltney had to explain that since Williams was the head coach of the team and, in essence, the primary reason the Tar Heels were in Phoenix, it was acceptable for him to use the bus to give his group a ride.

Under the organization of Eric Hoots, nearly three dozen former players and managers gathered at the team hotel on Saturday afternoon for an impromptu reunion. The current team and coaches saw the group when they were assembling for the pregame meal. "It made you realize how much of a family this is," said Luke Maye. "We hadn't even taken the court yet, and there were Danny Green and Vince Carter in our pregame meeting room. It shows how much people love coming back to Carolina. It's a testament to Coach Williams and to all the current and former players."

Williams has a way of making memories at the Final Four. In 1999, he'd attended the national semifinals in St. Petersburg, Florida. The official NABC hotel was a half hour away in Tampa, but gridlock hit the roads after the games. The head coach and his wife were wandering through the parking lot after the game, trying to figure out their way back to Tampa in an era with no Uber or cell phones, when a pair of brothers in a passing car rolled down their window.

"Hey Coach!" said a personable New Yorker named Lew Paskin. "I had Kansas in my pool!" The Jayhawks had lost to Kentucky in the second round.

The always-affable Williams approached the car and talked to Lew and his brother Mike. "Where are you headed?" Williams asked them.

"We're going to Tampa," the brothers replied. "You need a ride?"

Wanda Williams recoiled at the thought of accepting a ride from two complete strangers in the middle of Florida. But Roy Williams, who had hitchhiked home from Chapel Hill as a student, had made two new friends. The Paskin brothers drove the Williamses all the way back to their hotel, a drive that should have taken about 45 minutes but instead took approximately two hours due to traffic.

The brothers, diehard basketball fans who made the pilgrimage to the Final Four despite not having an official rooting interest, peppered Williams with questions the entire way. When they arrived at the hotel, they took a photo with him.

"Are you going to the game Monday night?" Williams asked. He was leav-

Theo Pinson lobbied CBS's Bill Raftery to provide one of his signature calls on a Pinson dunk. (Photo by J. D. Lyon Jr.)

Hubert Davis, C. B. McGrath, Roy Williams,
Brad Frederick, Eric Hoots, Steve Robinson, and
Sean May. (Photo by J. D. Lyon Jr.)

ing town, but the brothers were staying. That's when he handed them his tickets for the national championship game, which is how two loyal basketball fans ended up sitting on the same row as Grant Hill, Kevin Costner, and casino magnate Steve Wynn as Connecticut won the national title. "I think they were wondering what we did with Coach," Lew Paskin said.

The unexpected ride turned into a decades-long friendship. The next season, the Paskin brothers traveled to Lawrence for a game. Then they visited former Williams assistant coach Joe Holladay at a rodeo in his home state of Oklahoma. They journeyed to at least one Kansas game every year that Williams remained in Lawrence, then transferred their allegiances (and trips) to Chapel Hill when he returned to Carolina.

On one of their trips to the Smith Center, they were standing in the basketball office when they met legendary coach Dean Smith for the very first time. They introduced themselves and saw a twinkle of recognition in Smith's eyes. Their reputation had preceded them. "Hey," Smith said, "you're the guys who gave Roy a ride in Tampa."

The tickets always came courtesy of Williams, who always refused any of-

Joel Berry and Isaiah Hicks played video games in the locker room at the Final Four. (Photo by J. D. Lyon Jr.)

fers of payment. When the head coach was on his way to University of Phoenix Stadium on Saturday evening, he bumped into the Paskins. "You guys got your tickets OK?" he asked them.

"He's on his way to the Final Four, and he's worried about our tickets," Mike Paskin said. "He has the most integrity of anyone I know. He is a very real and genuine person."

■ Williams' experience coaching Kansas gave him a deep respect for Final Four opponent Oregon.

"Look," the head coach said, "if you beat Kansas in Kansas City, you're pretty doggone good." That's exactly what the Ducks had done, dismantling the Jayhawks in the regional final to earn a spot in the program's first Final Four since 1939.

While the rest of the Tar Heels struggled in the national semifinal, Meeks and Justin Jackson carried the team. Everyone other than that duo shot an abysmal 8-for-42 from the field. But Jackson scored 22 points and made three three-pointers, and Meeks was 11-for-13 from the field. With the Ducks

The notion of the Carolina Basketball family, a concept that has spanned generations, thrived during Dean Smith's 36 seasons as head coach and has continued in the two decades since. Players cherish the bonds of their brotherhood long after their college years have ended.

With that in mind, it was no surprise when dozens of former Tar Heel players came to Phoenix to cheer on the team against Oregon and Gonzaga, just as it made perfect sense for around 50 players to be on hand a year earlier at the Final Four in Houston.

The attendees in 2016 included NBA players Vince Carter, Harrison Barnes, Danny Green, and Wayne Ellington; coaches Shammond Williams, Wes Miller, King Rice, Brian Reese, and Jackie Manuel; and many other lettermen. The list in 2017 spanned the generations to include past Tar Heel heroes Lennie Rosenbluth, Mitch Kupchak, Al Wood, Pete Chilcutt, and George Lynch; current pros such as Carter and Green; and NBA administrators like Makhtar Ndiaye.

"I've noticed it," said Joel Berry II. "Guys come back, and they just treat you like you've known them for your whole lives. That's the greatest thing about this program. I'm going to take pride in [the fact] that Carolina is truly a brotherhood."

The 2016 and 2017 Final Fours weren't the only times Tar Heel alums have turned out to support their successors. Smaller groups were in St. Louis and Detroit to see Carolina win the 2005 and 2009 NCAA championships, for example. The overwhelming turnouts in Houston and Phoenix grew out of a dinner organized by Kenny Smith in 2015.

In the wake of the death of Dean Smith in February of that year, Kenny Smith assembled a group of Carolina alums attending the Final Four in Indianapolis.

"Kenny had this idea to bring us all together, have dinner and share stories about Coach Smith," Ndiaye

Roy Williams and former Tar Heel All-America and Turner Broadcasting analyst Kenny Smith. (Photo by J. D. Lyon Jr.)

said. "We're all family, and that's because of Coach Smith. We played for him, and Coach [Roy] Williams coached with him. Kenny wanted to reenergize that drive in the older guys to come back to campus more and support the current team to keep Coach Smith's principles alive."

A growing ring of former Tar Heel players soon emerged via texts, calls, emails, and visits. It started with alums from the 1990s like Jerry Stackhouse, Rasheed Wallace, Derrick Phelps, Carter, Shammond Williams, and Ndiaye and expanded to include players from previous decades, like J. R. Reid and others. They discuss the current team's season, successes by Tar Heels in the pros, and memories of times in Chapel Hill.

"There was no discussion beforehand about having a bunch of us former guys go to the Final Four in Houston or Phoenix," Ndiaye said. "It was just natural. We love each other and talk to each other all the time.

Former Tar Heels turned out by the dozens
in Houston in 2016 and again in Phoenix in 2017.
(Photo courtesy Makhtar Ndiaye)

We're all in touch as a larger group with lots of guys from different decades who never played with each other. We really have that family thing going on."

For an alum like Michael Brooker, who was recruited by Dean Smith but played for Bill Guthridge and Matt Doherty, the decision to put his life as a father, teacher, and prep coach on hold to fly to Phoenix was an easy one. Brooker drove 13 hours each way for the 2016 Final Four and attended all six 2017 Tar Heel NCAA contests.

(Photo courtesy Makhtar Ndiaye)

"I've been afforded so many wonderful relationships and experiences through my time at Carolina with the basketball program that I don't ever want to take the program for granted," he said. "Because of how things ended in Houston and what the guys went through losing that one, I wanted to be there in Phoenix to see them win it all."

"It means the world because you know [the former players] don't really know us, but we're family," Theo Pinson explained. "They'll take care of us no matter what. Just to see Vince Carter come two years in a row with everything that's going on. He's about to go into the playoffs, and he's making the effort to come here two years in a row to visit us. All those other guys coming down to see us means a lot, just to see how many people care. We're just carrying the tradition on. The guys who go to the Final Four after I leave will know where I'm going to be."

struggling to find open shots against Carolina's suffocating defense—Jackson had volunteered for defensive duty on Pac-12 Player of the Year Dillon Brooks, and limited him to 2-for-11 from the field—Carolina built a ten-point advantage with 8:31 remaining.

While impressed with his team's defense, Williams was still trying to cajole some offense out of them. During the media timeout with 7:48 left, the coach encouraged Berry, who had missed nine shots in a row and hadn't made a field goal in the second half. "Get your legs under you," Williams told Berry. "You're going to make the next one."

And so, after Pinson recovered a blocked Meeks shot with six minutes remaining, Berry was perfectly positioned outside the arc. Pinson found him with a pass, Berry got his legs under him, and the three-pointer swished through for a nine-point lead.

After making the shot, Berry turned and pointed at Williams, who pointed right back at the point guard.

"Over the years, Coach has challenged me in a way that has made me into the player I am today," Berry said. "When I hit that shot, it was a bigger message than what everyone else saw, because it showed the confidence that he has in me and the confidence he's had in me since I've been here. It's crazy what an impact he has on his players. That's why that was probably the most meaningful basket I've had since I've been here. It's something I will always remember. I was pointing at him because that's the man that took me in from my parents and made me into the player and the young man I am today."

Justin Jackson joined Joel Berry and
Kennedy Meeks on the All–Final Four team.
(Photo by Jeffrey A. Camarati)

The Carolina lead was still six points with 50 seconds left. But then, just like in the Kentucky game, it began to evaporate without warning. Oregon's Tyler Dorsey rolled in a three-pointer. Pinson missed a shot, and Keith Smith made a layup to cut the Carolina lead to 77–76.

With 5.8 seconds left, Oregon fouled Meeks deep in the backcourt. With the Ducks already in the double bonus, the Tar Heel senior would receive two free throws. He missed the first one short. Pinson, positioned next to Duck big man Jordan Bell, processed the miss. "When you miss one short, it's tough to come back from that," he said. "When it's long, the next one is probably going in. But when it's short, it's tough to recover."

"We tell them all the time that if they are lined up on the free-throw line, they are there to rebound," Williams said. "We want you thinking tip-out. Five guys are on the floor. One guy is thinking about making the free throw, and the other four are thinking tip-out. We show that to them all year long.

Kennedy Meeks tied his career high with 25 points in the Final Four against Oregon. (Photo by J. D. Lyon Jr.)

We give them bad grades if they don't go for the offensive rebound after a missed free throw."

Meeks' second shot was also short. Somehow, though, Pinson wriggled his way directly to the rim.

"When I came off the line when Kennedy shot it, I took a step," Pinson said. "And when I took a step, [Bell] did not touch me whatsoever. I was like, 'Wow.' He just stood there and tried to jump, but he jumped nonchalantly. I jumped as high as I could to tip it out, and I did."

Pinson's tip-out went directly to Berry near the top of the key. Oregon fouled the Tar Heel guard with 4.0 seconds remaining.

Meeks was distraught after the two misses. He crouched down near the baseline, petrified his final game would be remembered for two enormous errant free throws.

"I couldn't believe that I missed them," Meeks said. "I had a chance to win

Nate Britt hit a big three-pointer late in the first half against Oregon. (Photo by Jim Hawkins)

the game for my team, and I didn't do it. My teammates came over to me right away, though."

Pinson and Jackson pulled Meeks to his feet and embraced him. "Keep your head up," they told him. "We're going to win the game."

Meeks stopped feeling sorry for himself and started focusing on the final four seconds of the game. Berry, one of the team's best free-throw shooters, still had two free throws remaining.

His first shot, like Meeks', was short.

On the side of the lane, Meeks was now positioned next to Bell, who'd been beaten by Pinson for the previous offensive rebound.

"We were talking a little back and forth to each other," Meeks said. "He's one of the nicest guys on their team, but we definitely got into it a little bit. I told him there was no way they were winning this game. We had too much going for us, and we weren't going to lose."

Joel Berry struggled from the floor against Oregon but had 11 points and played solid defense. (Photo by Jim Hawkins)

Justin Jackson led UNC in scoring in the Final Four with 38 points, including 22 against Oregon. (Photo by J. D. Lyon Jr.)

Kennedy Meeks' rebound of a missed free throw secured the semifinal win for the Tar Heels. (Photo by Jamie Schwaberow/NCAA Photos)

Berry's second free throw was long, which should've given Bell the inside lane to the ball. But Meeks shouldered him deep under the rim, then somehow outworked a pair of Ducks to secure the rebound. Before Oregon could foul him, he tossed it outside the three-point line to Pinson, who ran out the clock.

It was one of the most unlikely possible endings to a Final Four game, but it was perfectly suited to Meeks' Tar Heel career. The rebound was his 14th of the game, to go with his 25 points. He'd missed an opportunity to seal the win in pretty fashion, but he recovered quickly enough to clinch the victory with a workmanlike, gritty rebound.

"The freshman Kennedy would not have made those plays," Britt said. "He's never been selfish, but it's been more of him doing what he thinks he needs to do and relying on that to make the team better. But over our last three or four games, he was 100 percent committed to doing whatever the team needed."

One of Roy Williams' signature traits as a coach has been his ability to

Theo Pinson

This is a priceless photo. Pizza is my favorite food, so of course I have a piece of pizza in my hand. Joel is my best friend. This is my dude for life. Of course we're right beside each other, and we're both on our phones. He is probably looking to see what Odell [Beckham] texted him, because that's his favorite player. I'm so glad I get to play another year with Joel. It's going to be a special season coming up.

Theo Pinson's offensive rebound in the final seconds helped UNC hold off the Ducks. (Photo by Ronald Martinez/Getty Images)

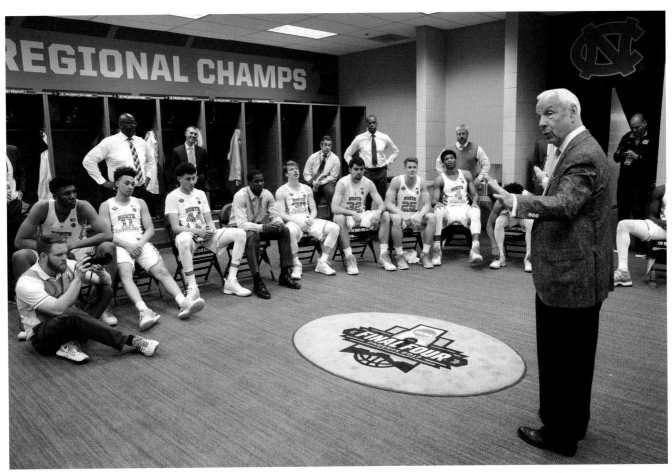

develop post players. He has coached All-Americas. He has coached first-round NBA Draft picks. He has coached National Players of the Year. He has coached Brice Johnson, Tyler Hansbrough, Tyler Zeller, and Sean May, whose jerseys now reside in the Smith Center rafters. He has made other players, including Ed Davis and Tony Bradley, into first-round NBA Draft picks. To have played in the post under Roy Williams is to have had some of the best possible tutelage for a big man.

Among that litany of standout big men, there is perhaps no one who consistently frustrated Williams more than Kennedy Meeks. And yet, as the head coach considered Meeks' performances against Kentucky and Oregon, on the doorstep of a national title, he was frank about the production of his senior.

"I have been a head coach for 29 years," Williams said. "I can't remember any post player playing at that level for two games in a row."

When the comment was relayed to Meeks, the senior's poker face twitched, then widened into a broad smile. "He said that?" Meeks asked. "Wow."

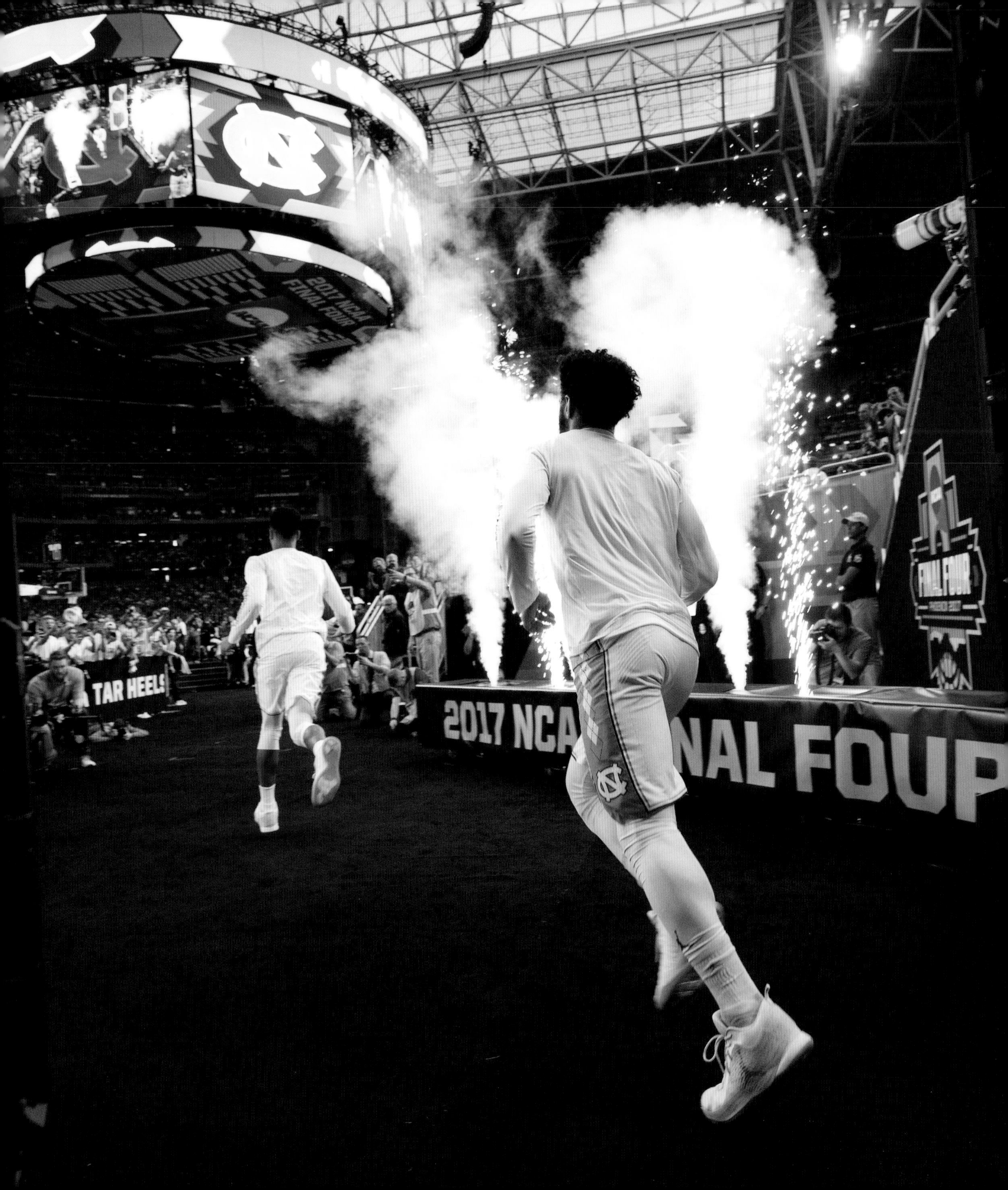
2017 NCAA FINAL FOUR
TAR HEELS
2017 NCA NAL FOUR
FINAL FOUR

Well after midnight the Sunday evening before Monday's national championship game, Kennedy Meeks was searching YouTube. Meeks stayed up until 3:00 A.M. searching for videos of Gonzaga post man Przemek Karnowski. The seven-foot-one, 300-pound center was evidence that the Zags were different from most Tar Heel opponents: they were as committed to the inside game as Carolina was.

Meeks clicked through numerous videos, trying to learn Karnowski's game. In most cases, the Tar Heels had a history with virtually every opponent. They'd played against them in an AAU game or watched them on television multiple times. But Karnowski was from Poland, and Meeks had very little background on him other than what was provided in the UNC scouting report. He wanted to learn tendencies and understand Karnowski's game.

Meanwhile, Justin Jackson texted Kenny Williams, who was sidelined with a knee injury. The sophomore had been a key part of Carolina's success early in the year but had been forced to watch the postseason run from the bench. Jackson knew Williams had occasionally struggled with the conflicting emotions of being thrilled at his team's success while being frustrated that he couldn't personally participate.

"I've got you," Jackson wrote to Williams. "We're going to do this for you."

Down the hall, Joel Berry II was sitting in his bed. At the team's late-night snack on Sunday night, Roy Williams told the players, "Visualize who you're going to run up to and hug when that clock hits zero tomorrow night."

Players talked about the possible thrill of the moment while they sat in the meeting room. That night, Berry knew exactly how he wanted the celebration to unfold.

"I visualized myself hugging Theo and hugging Justin," he said. "We came in together [as freshmen], and we said we wanted to help this team win a national championship."

The trio was special to Williams because they committed at a time when Carolina was dealing with numerous outside issues. Recruiting is sacred to Williams. He loves the chase and loves building relationships with players and their families. He is proud of the University of North Carolina and has always loved introducing it to prospects.

At the time Pinson, Jackson, and Berry committed, though, he was having trouble even getting players to visit campus. This was a completely new phenomenon for him. Williams had lost players before, but he always was able to at least get them on campus to give his best recruiting pitch. When players didn't visit, he felt he wasn't even in the game. He estimated that for a couple of seasons, over half the prospects he invited to visit turned down the opportunity to come to Chapel Hill.

Williams is legendarily competitive. He competes at everything. Steve Robinson has a favorite story about walking up to a locked Smith Center

12
CHAMPIONS

Joel Berry became the first Tar Heel ever to make two All–Final Four teams.
(Photo by J. D. Lyon Jr.)

Carolina was all smiles during the team's bus ride to the shootaround on the day of the final game. (Photo by J. D. Lyon Jr.)

with Williams, and Williams racing to see who could get his key in the lock first. Friends know that with very rare exceptions, they will always flip a coin to determine who pays for dinner when they go on a trip with Williams. On a five-day trip like the annual Phoenix jaunt, that means that a run of bad luck could result in paying for a half dozen meals. But there's no avoiding it— those are the ground rules. When the Hall of Fame announced Williams as the newest member in April 2007 at the Final Four in Atlanta, he celebrated with lunch at the local hamburger institution the Varsity. When it was time to pay the bill, of course, the next step was clear. "Let's flip for it," the world's newest Hall of Famer said.

Williams was once on a trip with close friend Cody Plott when the duo began discussing Carolina quarterback Darian Durant. They disagreed about whether he was a junior or a senior. "Wanna bet?" Williams asked Plott. A call to Chapel Hill confirmed that Plott was correct. Williams paid his debt with a five-dollar bill, on which he wrote: "I lost to you, jerk." Plott still carries it in his wallet.

With the climate around Tar Heel recruiting in the mid-2010s, Williams felt he wasn't even able to compete. He could handle—poorly—losing. He couldn't handle not even being in the contest.

That's why he was so devoted to Pinson, Berry, and Jackson. The coach prizes loyalty, and all three had demonstrated it. "All three of them committed to us during their junior year," he said. "The NCAA stuff started to come out after their junior year, and they stuck with us. Not only did they sign with us in the fall of their senior years, but they never asked for a release. That group right there withstood more negativity than any other group and has been the core of two straight national championship–game teams."

The trio was committed to Williams, but they were also committed to each other. They had been one of the most tightknit recruiting classes in the Williams era. It began with texts to each other and grew at camps and all-star events before they ever arrived on campus. During a preseason trip to the Bahamas the first month of their freshman season, the trio put their arms around each other and shared a moment on the court.

"One of these days," they told each other, "it will be our time to take this program to the highest level."

"We talked about this being what we came to Carolina for," Jackson said. "We said, 'Let's put our mark on this program.' We were extremely excited about what we could do here. I don't know if we necessarily thought we'd be able to do what we have done, but we knew we would be able to do some big things. That was the start of us saying, 'Let's go do this.'"

Almost three years later, Pinson and Berry knew Jackson would be playing his final game for the Tar Heels against Gonzaga. His stellar junior campaign meant he would be a high first-round NBA Draft selection. The trio that had come in together in the Bahamas promising big things wanted to send Jackson out exactly as they had often dreamed.

■ If Steve Robinson had been nervous about his team's mindset before the national semifinal against Oregon, he quickly learned the Tar Heels were much more relaxed going into the national championship game.

The Tar Heels boarded the bus for University of Phoenix Stadium for Monday's shootaround in their usual fashion. Players were in the back, Williams was in the front right seat, and everyone else filled in the middle.

Robinson was one of the final people to board. He escaped notice for a few minutes, but finally, at the shootaround, the players began laughing. The assistant coach was wearing green shorts. For reasons no one has yet been able to fully explain, this struck the players as hilarious.

"When he got on the bus, no one really realized it," said Joel Berry. "And then all of a sudden, it hit everybody at the same time. Everyone said, 'Coach Rob, what are you wearing? That's nowhere near our colors.' It was closer to Oregon colors."

"You know what, Coach Rob?" Berry told the assistant. "That's your last time wearing those shorts. After this, you need to take them and throw them away."

> We talked about this being what we came to Carolina for. We were extremely excited about what we could do here. I don't know if we necessarily thought we'd be able to do what we have done, but we knew we would be able to do some big things.
>
> —JUSTIN JACKSON

Assistant coach Steve Robinson broke out the green shorts for the final shootaround of the season. (Photo by J. D. Lyon Jr.)

Robinson is Williams' longest-tenured assistant and is typically one of the most fashionable coaches on the staff. The rare misstep tickled the team.

"He said his wife gave them to him," Berry said. "So I have some sympathy for him. But at the same time, I never want to see those shorts again."

Roy Williams didn't care about Robinson's fashion choices, but he was thrilled with the impact that day's selection of shorts had on his team. He joined in the ribbing and cultivated a lighthearted mood throughout the shootaround.

The West Coast location for the game meant an unusual 6:00 P.M. start time, and he wanted to give the players one singular thought as they tried to pass the upcoming hours before their regular pregame routine began. The Tar Heels gathered around the center jump circle at University of Phoenix Stadium.

"One team is going to win tonight," Williams told them. "You are here because you are good enough to win it. You played your way here. Only one team is going to enjoy themselves tonight, so why not let it be us? You got here last year, and you had a great experience. Let's be the last team standing."

Gonzaga's lineup on the white board in the team room during the team's breakfast at the UNC hotel. (Photo by J. D. Lyon Jr.)

A trio of former Tar Heel standouts—Brendan Haywood, Hubert Davis, and Sean May—shared a moment before tipoff. (Photo by J. D. Lyon Jr.)

Theo Pinson's dunk provided the first points of the title game. (Photo by Jeffrey A. Camarati)

■ On the very first Carolina basket of the championship game, Pinson finally got his NCAA Tournament dunk. Raftery and play-by-play man Jim Nantz audibly chuckled on the national television broadcast. "There's the dunk he's been waiting for all tournament long!" Nantz said. Raftery, undoubtedly thrilling the Pinson family, gave him a "Send it in, Theo!" call. The rest of the Tar Heel baskets would not be so easy.

Back in September, Williams had reminded his team of the little plays they wished they had made against Villanova. Early in the championship game against Gonzaga, they showed that they remembered. After an errant Zags shot, the ball appeared to be batted out of bounds. But Pinson chased the ball across the baseline and kept it alive just long enough for Hicks to also dive across the baseline, hurling it back to a waiting Meeks.

The play signified everything Carolina had worked for since the disappointing ending in Houston and was the kind of effort play that Gonzaga might not yet realize was necessary in a championship game.

"We could have easily let the ball go out of bounds and just played defense," Meeks said. "But we didn't. I think that's all about being motivated. That's all about not wanting to lose again, and about having another opportunity on a big stage. We all felt if we were given another chance to win a national championship game, we weren't going to lose."

The Tar Heels had to get every loose ball, because their recent shooting woes continued. Carolina hit just 30.6 percent of its field goals in the first half, with Berry's nine points the team high. A quick spurt out of the locker room gave the Heels a five-point lead, but a turnover spurred a six-point Gonzaga run.

Jackson's stellar defense on an opposing star again was essential. This time, he defended Nigel Williams-Goss, harassing him into 5-for-17 shooting for the game and 3-for-11 in the second half. During one stretch in the final stanza, Williams-Goss missed five shots in a row.

"I'll be honest," Jackson said. "I've never been as tired as I was in the

Kennedy Meeks averaged 12.2 points and shot 64.3 percent from the field in the NCAA Tournament. (Photo by Jeffrey A. Camarati)

(opposite)
Joel Berry scored a game-high 22 points in the national championship game win over Gonzaga. (Photo by Jeffrey A. Camarati)

Gonzaga game. Ever. That was a culmination of the Oregon game and the Gonzaga game. But I was just trying to leave everything out there, and I knew the rest of my teammates would do the same. And that's how we got to where we were."

Berry had not shot well in the Oregon game, making just two of his 14 field goals and going only two-for-eight from the three-point line. But teammates and coaches considered him one of the most reliable shooters on the team. His three-point shooting battles with Jackson in practice were legendary within the locker room.

Last season, Williams had introduced the duo, along with Marcus Paige, to a game played by Golden State's Steph Curry and Klay Thompson. The object was simple: shoot three-pointers for as long as you can without missing two in a row. A normal person might go a handful of shots before missing twice. A very good basketball player could get into the dozens. Jackson, Berry, and Paige often went into triple figures.

Isaiah Hicks came up big on both ends of the floor against the Zags. (Photo by J. D. Lyon Jr.)

"Coach was trying to find a way that we could have a little bit of competition to help us be able to shoot a higher percentage," Berry said. "Over the summertime, we put up so many shots, and I think all of that is what contributed to us hitting all of those three's that we made this year."

Jackson and Berry had taken to jokingly calling each other the "Splash Bros," echoing the nickname given to Curry and Thompson. So despite the recent shooting struggles, there was no hesitation when Pinson fired a bullet pass to Berry on the left wing. The junior guard stepped into his shot and drilled a guarded three-pointer for a short-lived two-point lead with four minutes left. Williams-Goss responded with his best stretch of the game, scoring eight straight points for the Zags. Gonzaga led 65–63 with 1:50 remaining.

Pinson, once again the playmaker, threaded an almost impossible pass to Jackson for a bucket and a foul. "We have nobody else on our team who would have made that play," Williams said of Pinson's pass. "There's no question. That's who he is."

Jackson also converted the free throw to give Carolina the lead. And after a defensive stop, a Meeks offensive rebound prolonged a Tar Heel possession just long enough for Hicks to drive from the top of the key and make a contested basket that provided three points of breathing room.

Joel Berry even tossed in a jump hook in the title game. (Photo by J. D. Lyon Jr.)

No one realized Hicks was playing on a painful leg injury, the result of catching an errant knee to his thigh. By late Monday night after the game, he was no longer able to put weight on the leg. A week later, he had to have the leg drained to relieve significant fluid buildup.

"When my adrenaline was pumping, I didn't think about it," Hicks said. "But once the game was over, I felt terrible." When it mattered, however, he didn't feel terrible.

With under 20 seconds left, a still-fresh Meeks, in his 22nd minute of action, swatted away a Williams-Goss shot. Berry snatched the rebound and saw Jackson sprinting for the rim.

Berry lofted a pass. As he let it go, he thought, "We are really about to win the national championship." Jackson dunked it home, sparking pandemonium on the Tar Heel bench. Gonzaga raced back downcourt again, but Meeks made yet another big play, intercepting a cross-court pass and shoveling it to Berry just before a Zags foul with 7.3 seconds on the clock.

"That steal," Meeks said with a wide smile, "was all my defensive back skills."

After the foul, Berry sprinted to the sideline in front of the Tar Heel Sports Network radio crew—almost exactly the same location where Kris Jenkins had celebrated his title-clinching shot the year before. All over the court,

Lennie Rosenbluth (1957), Sam Perkins (1982), George Lynch (1993), Marvin Williams (2005), and Bobby Frasor (2009)

What were your general observations about the 2017 Tar Heels?

WILLIAMS: From the beginning of the year, they seemed to use the way last year ended as motivation to get back to the national championship and win it this time. Their experience definitely played a major role in their success.

FRASOR: I thought they would compete for the ACC championship, but I didn't think with losing Brice [Johnson] and Marcus [Paige] it would be a Final Four or national championship team. I guess I am a terrible predictor. I didn't know how much Justin [Jackson], Joel [Berry], and Kennedy [Meeks] would have improved from last year. They were very talented, and as most of Coach Williams' teams, they got stronger and stronger.

Was there anything about this team that reminded you of your national championship season?

ROSENBLUTH: Most definitely: the rebounding and playing together. Looking for each other, really playing together and tremendous hustle. We both had a strong desire to win.

LYNCH: We played totally different. Coach Smith would have pulled his hair out seeing some of the shots that Coach Williams lets them shoot. But I'm not in their locker room, so it's easy to be an armchair coach. He had to believe in the style they were playing. He had to know that we were going to outlast them, had to believe in his bench, and had to believe that we were going inside. Coach Williams continues to believe that going inside first, like Coach Smith believed in going through our big guys, is the way to success.

What motivated your team when you won the national championship?

ROSENBLUTH: We didn't want to lose. We felt somewhere along the line someone would make a mistake and we would capitalize on it and we would win. The same thing happened like in the [2017] Oregon game, we missed the foul shots late, but from that outside position we came in and got the rebound and tipped it back out. That's just tremendous hustle and heart. You learn in junior high school about boxing out, and here's college All-Americas not doing that and our guys coming in and getting that rebound. It's all desire.

WILLIAMS: We just wanted to win. We had great upperclassmen that wanted to end their careers on top. Their leadership was the reason we were able to pull it off.

LYNCH: The scheduling played out right for us. It was always self-motivation. We lost to Michigan in December, and we thought we should have won, we thought we were better than them. We went on a big winning streak in the ACC but went into Wake Forest not ready to play, and Coach decided to take the starters out and teach us a lesson, so we lost that game by a lot. Losing to Georgia Tech in the ACC Tournament kind of refocused us. Derrick Phelps was hurt and he thought he let us down by not being able to play. He said we wouldn't lose again, and we didn't. In the Final Four, we got to play Kansas, who we'd lost to in 1991, and Michigan, and that gave us an edge. We had extra incentive not to lose to those teams again.

PERKINS: One was to win it for Coach Smith. We had come so close to beating Bobby Knight in the

Bobby Frasor was co-captain in 2009 when Carolina
beat Michigan State by 17 points in the title game. (Photo by
Jeffrey A. Camarati)

Final Four and winning it the year before, and our leader, Jimmy Black, and guys like James [Worthy] wanted to make sure we finished it this time. Since we knew what to expect the second time, there was greater determination to win it all.

What do you remember most about winning the national championship?

ROSENBLUTH: For us it was just another game. We expected to win and didn't realize the implications of it then. We just kept on winning like we did all year. Our manager, Joel Fleishman, put the trophy in the bag with the dirty uniforms and brought it back to Chapel Hill.

WILLIAMS: Hugging Coach Williams after we won and thanking him a million times for giving me the opportunity to play for him and Carolina. I chose Carolina because we had a chance to win, so I was grateful he gave me that chance.

LYNCH: It was all a blur. You go to Carolina to graduate and win a national championship, but you don't appreciate it until now. I thought we should go to the Final Four every year, but it's harder than you think.

PERKINS: Winning was surreal. It was a rare opportunity to get there twice. To win one was very special for your school pride; it was why you went to Carolina. We held it really sacred because it was a once-in-a-lifetime opportunity. It was something everybody wanted for the school. They can never take that from you. You are recognized as a college champion for all time.

What advice would you give this year's team about how special it is to be a national champion?

ROSENBLUTH: Stay together, be together. Someone on that team be the man to call everybody and know, as years go by, what everyone is doing. Always stay together, and you become more than teammates— you become brothers. You all did something extraordinary, and don't lose each other as the years go by.

LYNCH: As you get older and you have your own kids, it's cool to be part of a championship because they can hear people talk about their father's accomplishments. More than anything, I want my son to learn the hard work and commitment it takes to be a Tar Heel. If he learns that, then I'll be a proud father. As great as UNC is, we have six national titles, and to be part of that small group— to know that there is a small group of us who hung a national championship banner—is very special.

FRASOR: Coach asked me to speak to the team the night before the Gonzaga game, and I told them only a few teams have a seat at the upper echelon of Carolina teams. I hit on that point. The Family is amazing, but if you win, you have a special seat at that table. They can always come back to Chapel Hill and point up to that banner.

Marvin Williams hit the game-winning shot for the Tar Heels in the 2005 national championship game against Illinois. (Photo by Jeffrey A. Camarati)

C. B. McGrath and Hubert Davis (right) erupted on the sideline late in the game against Gonzaga. (Photo by Ronald Martinez/Getty Images)

the Tar Heels were realizing the moment. At least four players were in tears. Meeks wrapped Williams in an enormous hug, the type usually reserved for after the final outcome.

"You could see he was full of emotion," Meeks said. "We've been through a lot, and most of it was from my wrongdoings, whether on or off the court. He's the one who made me a man. That hug was for being grateful for all the opportunities, for putting me in the right positions, and for being the greatest coach I'll ever be around. Brice said he's a role model for him. That's what he is for me, too. He's been a major figure in my life who I will always remember."

Of course, the duo could only finish their on-court relationship in one way: with Williams barking at Meeks. "Finish the game!" the coach told his player.

"I had never seen that before," Williams said of his players' displays of

emotion with time still on the clock. "It was a little scary to me, because there were so many things that could still happen."

Meeks' fellow senior was one of the players who was overwhelmed.

"After Kennedy made that block, I got a little emotional," Hicks said. "I couldn't hold it back, and the game was still going on. I was out there, but I couldn't see. Then I saw Kennedy had stolen it again, and that's when it really hit me. It's over. We did it. It was starting to sink in. We went to back-to-back Final Fours, we went to back-to-back national championship games, we lost one and now we've won this one. As Joel was shooting his free throws, I thought, 'Man, this is crazy.'"

Isaiah Hicks gave UNC a 68–65 lead with this basket with 26 seconds to play. (Photo by Mark J. Rebilas/USA Today Sports Images)

As Berry toed the free-throw line, he realized his eyes were wet. He looked around and saw Hicks and Meeks in tears. "I've got to get myself together," Berry thought to himself. "I'm about to shoot two free throws."

A game official slid beside him. "Your coach wants to know if you need a timeout," the referee said.

Berry was distracted. "What?" he said.

"Your coach wants to know if you need a timeout," the referee repeated.

"Oh," Berry said. "Yes I do!"

The Tar Heels took a 30-second timeout. Teammates, battling their own emotions, were equally amazed to see the usually stalwart Berry in tears. "None of us," Hicks said, "had ever seen Joel like that."

It was perhaps the rawest emotions ever displayed by Carolina players while a basketball game still had time on the clock. Jackson managed to keep his composure until the buzzer, but just barely. Virtually everyone else was welling up.

Kennedy Meeks' block with 15 seconds to play helped clinch the national title for the Tar Heels. (Photo by Bob Donnan/USA Today Sports Images)

"I was crying as I came to the sideline," Pinson said. "It was crazy. I'm holding my jersey, and I'm like, 'Dude, you've got to keep it together. What are you doing? There are seven seconds to go.' You can't even explain that feeling. The fact that we knew we did it and we had won."

Berry hugged Williams. "Coach, I'm about to lose it," he said to the Hall of Famer.

"You're going to go up there and knock in these two free throws," Williams told him. "Then we're going to get back on defense, and we're going to win the game. And then you can do whatever you want to do."

"When we walked back on the court, everybody was looking at each other with tears in our eyes," Pinson said. "We were like, 'Oh my goodness, we are a mess.'"

Berry went back to the line, but the 30 seconds hadn't settled him. As he eyed the goal, he realized it was still blurry. He missed the first one, then collected himself. "I'm not going to miss two free throws because I'm crying," he told himself as he stood at the line in front of 76,168 fans. He wiped his eyes and made the second one, providing the final 71–65 margin.

The Zags missed one last meaningless three-pointer. Pinson collected the rebound and flung the ball toward the roof—or maybe the ceiling. The Tar Heels celebrated on the court as streamers, slightly delayed compared to the previous year's instantaneous eruption, fired from the rafters. Tears flowed.

"It's such a weird feeling," Jackson said. "You can't control it. It's pure happiness, but it's just tears."

In the hysteria, Berry, Jackson, and Pinson found each other.

"I went up to Theo and I said, 'This is what we came here for,'" Berry said. "And then I went to Justin and I said the same thing. To see that celebration was the best thing. It is something I will remember for the rest of my life. Even when I can't remember anything else, I will still remember that celebration."

(opposite)
Justin Jackson's dunk with 12 seconds to play gave UNC a five-point cushion.
(Photo by Chris Steppig/USA Today Sports Images)

Justin Jackson was overcome with emotion as the Tar Heels won the national championship. (Photo by J. D. Lyon Jr.)

(Photo by Jeffrey A. Camarati)

The postgame panorama was surreal, especially when contrasted with the scene one year earlier in Houston. This time, for the first time ever, Wanda Williams made her way to the court to celebrate with her husband. Roy Williams shares a ritual with Wanda and his immediate family: just before tipoff of every game, he finds them in the stands and gives them a quick wave. But Wanda had always resisted being part of the postgame festivities.

This time, she brought Scott and Kimberly, along with Aiden and Court. The little ones made snow angels in the growing pile of confetti. The family watched "One Shining Moment" together on the podium, as Roy Williams wrapped his arms around his grandsons.

In the immediate moments after the final buzzer, Williams had slipped his 2009 championship ring off of his right ring finger and put it in his pocket. Other than for specific recruiting purposes, he did not wear a ring on his right hand again for the rest of the spring and summer. "I'm waiting to get the one this team earned," he said.

Pinson sprinted to his parents in the stands, where they shared an emotional embrace. Two months earlier, they'd been concerned that his season was over. "I told you we were going to do it," Pinson said through his sobs. "Thank you for supporting me through everything."

Tears flowed everywhere. Hubert Davis crawled into the family section and embraced his kids and wife, Leslie.

After cutting down both nets, the team began to make their way through the cavernous University of Phoenix Stadium. Last year, the walk had been a long one. This year, the locker room was almost directly off the court.

Tony Bradley was one of the first players into the tunnel. He was dealing with cramping issues, and as soon as he reached the locker room, he laid down on the floor. "I didn't want to get in the way of the celebration," he told his teammates.

It didn't work. Like a bunch of joyous toddlers, they piled on top of him, a happy mass of Tar Heels on the floor with one seven-footer on the bottom of the heap.

Roy Williams, meanwhile, had become a more savvy celebrator. His team's victory parties had typically included their traditional jumping around, followed by the head coach writing the number of teams remaining in the tournament—now just one—on the locker-room white board.

During the course of the postseason, however, his players had added water to the celebration ritual, and he had gotten soaked after the win over Kentucky. With the players inside the locker room and Williams the last member of the team to enter, he paused just outside the door, knowing what was coming next. He took off his Alexander Julian suit jacket, one that soon would have a home in the Carolina Basketball Museum alongside the program's

13
REDEEMED

Joel Berry became the first player since Bill Walton in 1973 to score 20 points in consecutive title games. (Photo by Bob Donnan/USA Today Sports Images)

The Oregon and Gonzaga games ended in similar fashion, with Theo Pinson tossing the ball into the air to cap a Tar Heel victory. (Photo by J. D. Lyon Jr.)

Seniors Kanler Coker and Isaiah Hicks. (Photo by J. D. Lyon Jr.)

Kennedy Meeks
with Aaron Rohlman,
Seventh Woods,
and Stilman White.
(Photo by J. D. Lyon Jr.)

Best friends Joel
Berry and Theo
Pinson in tears after
winning the NCAA
title. (Photo by Brett
Wilhelm/NCAA
Photos)

Theo Pinson averaged 8.5 rebounds in the Final Four wins.

(Photo by J. D. Lyon Jr.)

2017 Managers Emily Brickner, Tyler Hagan, John Bumgarner, Chase Bengel, Forrest Reynolds, and Maria Vanderford. (Photo by J. D. Lyon Jr.)

sixth NCAA championship trophy, three of which had now come under Williams' watch.

He walked into the locker room in his shirtsleeves and was promptly drenched by his happy players.

The previous year, Jordan had joined him in the locker room. This year, however, Jordan was watching the game at home. The famously superstitious Tar Heel great had told the equally superstitious Williams he was concerned he had been a jinx in 2016.

Jordan texted Williams as soon as the game was over, and the coach shared the message with his team. "I'm so happy for you and the team," it read. "You raised the ceiling to the roof tonight."

There are a few stages of winning a championship. There's the jubilation. There's the satisfaction. And then there was that moment just after Williams talked to the Tar Heels, as everyone was left with their own thoughts about

Kennedy Meeks finished his career with 1,052 rebounds, fifth-most in UNC history. (Photo by J. D. Lyon Jr.)

Roy Williams shared the spotlight with his grandsons, Aiden and Court, in the aftermath of the championship game victory. (Photo by J. D. Lyon Jr.)

Senior manager Forrest Reynolds. (Photo by J. D. Lyon Jr.)

(Photo by J. D. Lyon Jr.)

Roy Williams placed one of the Phoenix Stadium nets around the neck of senior forward Isaiah Hicks. (Photo by J. D. Lyon Jr.)

(L) Justin Jackson and Kenny Williams.
(Photo by J. D. Lyon Jr.)

(R) (Photo by J. D. Lyon Jr.)

what had just happened. The coach made his way around the room, relishing the moment with a team that had just etched itself into Carolina Basketball history.

"We had a conversation after the game, and Coach told me how much I've meant to this program and how much I've meant to him," said Kennedy Meeks. "I could tell that he was proud of me. When you reflect and look back at the past seasons, everything is to make you better. In this program, if you listen to everything Coach says, you will be successful. The Lord has a plan, and Coach was definitely part of that plan."

Fans swarmed the team hotel, the Kimpton Palomar, to welcome back the 2017 national champions. Hundreds lined the steps leading to the second-floor lobby, where hotel employees roped off a pathway for players to make their way to the elevators.

Upstairs, the Britt family gathered in their hotel room. One year earlier,

Brandon Robinson did the honors of soaking Coach Williams when he entered the locker room following the Gonzaga game. (Photo by J. D. Lyon Jr.)

Roy Williams became the sixth coach in NCAA history to win three national championships. (Photo by J. D. Lyon Jr.)

(Photo by J. D. Lyon Jr.)

Nate Britt Sr. had been one of the last people to see Roy Williams on the night of the championship game. After Williams had consoled every friend and spoken to every well-wisher in the team meeting room following Carolina's loss to Villanova, he walked to the elevator at the Hilton Post Oak. The doors opened, and out walked the elder Britt, the adopted father of the player who had just plunged a blade into the Tar Heels. "You did a great job with this team," Britt Sr. said to Williams. The two men embraced. "I didn't want it to happen," Williams told him. "But I couldn't be happier for you and Kris. This is a great night for your family."

Nate Britt

I never could have imagined this picture. Growing up, whenever Kris or I won something, the other would want to do the exact same thing. Even when we played on the same team, we would always try to outplay each other. It's always been a competition. Anytime one of us gets an award, the other one wants to get it the next year.

But who could have imagined we would do that with a national championship? Kris standing there in Carolina gear makes this picture even more unbelievable. I'm sure people on the outside probably don't understand it. But this is just how our family is. We support each other to the end. So it seems normal to me that Kris would put how I feel in front of how Villanova fans might feel. It felt completely natural for him to come support his brother, and to be happy for us when we won the title.

Roy Williams has many sayings he frequently sprinkles through messages to his team, and one of his favorites is: "The eye in the sky don't lie." Translation for a college basketball player: "Let me show you the videotape."

Williams spent 10 years as an assistant coach under Dean Smith, who built a Hall of Fame career by meticulously preparing for almost any scenario his players might face in a game. Himself a 2007 Naismith Basketball Hall of Fame inductee, Williams has won more than a few games in his 29 years as a head coach by focusing on the details.

Some college basketball observers have tagged his Tar Heel teams as fast-break, high-scoring machines that have less success on the defensive end of the court. Ironically, though, it's rebounding, defense, and paying attention to those pesky details that have won the Tar Heels national titles under Williams in 2005, 2009, and 2017.

UNC has allowed 71, 70, 69, 72, 76, and 65 points in the six Final Four wins in those three championship seasons. Five of the six opponents—including Illinois and Gonzaga in the 2005 and 2017 title games, respectively—shot less than 40 percent from the floor. The Zags came into the championship game averaging 83.1 points and shooting 50.8 percent, but the Tar Heels held them to 18 points below their average and 33.9 percent from the floor in UNC's 71–65 victory.

"Coach preached all year we're not going to get to the last Monday night if we are not good defensively," said NCAA South Regional MVP Luke Maye. "We struggled at some points during the year, but he continued to tell us after every game that defense wins championships. For us to play at the end of the year the way he talks about all the time—diving on the floor, getting loose balls, rebounding, tipping out—is a testament to him. He's been there before, and he knows what it takes."

The 2017 national championship banner will hang

Justin Jackson became the third Tar Heel to win ACC Player-of-the-Year honors and an NCAA title in the same year. (Photo by J. D. Lyon Jr.)

in the Smith Center in Chapel Hill rather than in an arena in Lexington, Kentucky; Eugene, Oregon; or Spokane, Washington, because of numerous plays like the ones Williams and his staff focus on in every practice, every film session, and every meeting—plays like Maye and Kennedy Meeks diving on the floor for loose balls against Kentucky and Oregon; Meeks getting the ball inbounds before Kentucky coach John Calipari could signal for a timeout; Theo Pinson attacking the Wildcat defense before it could get set up before Maye's game-winning jumper; and Pinson securing an offensive rebound in the waning moments

Carolina held both Oregon and Gonzaga under
40 percent shooting from the floor in the Final Four.
(Photo by Jeffrey A. Camarati)

of the national semifinals by tipping out a missed
free throw rather than trying to grab the rebound by
himself.

The little things that Williams harped on all year,
and in all years, became the difference between
winning and losing a national championship.

"It's tough for us," Pinson said with a laugh,
"because it worked. You can't say anything about it
because what he tells us, it worked. If you want to
win, you do it and you win. Those plays are the things
he's been preaching to us since day one. I could have
grabbed the ball in the Oregon game—I was so high.

Theo Pinson's drive and pass to Luke Maye was one of the greatest full-court plays leading to a basket in UNC basketball history. (Photo by J. D. Lyon Jr.)

But what we've been taught to do is to tip it out, and that killed a couple of seconds. I saw Joel [Berry] and hit it right to him."

Consensus All-America and ACC Player of the Year Justin Jackson sums up Williams' attention to detail in this way: "Everything he always says is extremely important, and those things turn out to be the things that his teams are best at. As the NCAA Tournament went on, we were at the best point of our game when it came to defense. Everything that coach says will translate to the game does translate. That's huge. And he gets everybody to buy into that."

Players watched a replay of the game's final moments in the locker room on Eric Hoots' laptop. (Photo by J. D. Lyon Jr.)

In 2016, Britt had FaceTimed with Jenkins at the hotel after the game, not wanting to subject his teammates to a potentially awkward in-person meeting. This time, Jenkins was in the room with the family, wearing a brand-new Carolina national champions t-shirt. Britt's sister, along with his aunt and uncle, plus his parents and Jenkins, joined them.

The family joined hands and gave thanks for the incredible blessings they had received as a family. Two seasons. Two national championships. One unforgettable shot. One amazing redemption.

Which reminded Britt there was still some business that needed attending. That team group chat, the one titled "Redemption." The title was no longer appropriate. He altered it to "Redeemed."

■ Williams was busy receiving congratulations instead of condolences like last year. His post-championship parties had evolved. In 2005 in St. Louis, after he won his first national title, family and friends gathered in his hotel

Coach Williams and Joel Berry check out a text message following the game. (Photo by J. D. Lyon Jr.)

Coach Williams read a text message from Michael Jordan to the team on the bus on the way back to the hotel. (Photo by J. D. Lyon Jr.)

A massive throng of Carolina fans met the team at the hotel in downtown Phoenix. (Photo by J. D. Lyon Jr.)

suite. Around midnight, he realized no one had anything to eat. The coach and his wife ordered pizza for the group. Then, after the celebration wound down, the couple and their children went around the room cleaning up pizza boxes.

In 2009 in Detroit, the team hotel was so small there was little room for a party. In 2017, though, the team meeting room provided plenty of space— and sufficient food—to celebrate. This time, though, with Aiden and Court getting sleepy, it might have been the earliest night of any of the three titles. By 12:30 A.M., as Franklin Street in Chapel Hill was still roaring, the festivities were mostly over for the Williams family in Phoenix.

Williams had time to reflect on his incredible good fortune, but also on

In June, Justin Jackson was the 15th pick in the first round of the NBA Draft. (Photo by J. D. Lyon Jr.)

some very important people whom he missed. Dean Smith had been in the locker room after the 2005 championship. Bill Guthridge's wry smile had been a part of every Tar Heel NCAA title since 1982. One of Williams' closest friends, Ted Seagroves, had passed away from pancreatic cancer in 2014. His mother was always on his mind.

He felt fortunate to be able to celebrate with his grandchildren. But he also felt the absence of those he knew would relish the evening.

"Teddy would have loved the ride this year and last year," Williams said. "He made my life better and easier because he could add some comic relief

The team enjoyed watching the festivities at the Smith Center and overhead shots of their bus ride home from the RDU airport. (Photo by J. D. Lyon Jr.)

when I needed it, and that part has been missing the last couple of years. Coach Guthridge and Coach Smith really would have loved this team. As players, they were overachievers, and they liked those kinds of guys. Dee Rowe [former Connecticut coach] sent me a very nice note that said Coach Smith and Bill really enjoyed the Gonzaga game."

■ The team arrived back in Chapel Hill the next day to an adoring reception. Another member of the 1982 team, Sam Perkins, had sought out Williams in Phoenix. Perkins, whom Williams calls "Bruce" because it's his middle name, had also been in Houston. This time was a much happier occasion, and Perkins and Williams reminisced about the 1982 team's return to Chapel Hill. On that journey, the bus detoured down Franklin Street, where fans lined the road to cheer the Tar Heels. Several players climbed out of the emergency exit on the top of the bus and sat on the bus, waving to the fans.

"You probably don't know this," Perkins told Williams, "but I almost fell off the bus when I was sitting up there."

"That right there," Williams said with a grin, "decided that the players were going to stay inside the bus when we went down Franklin Street."

Justin Jackson danced once more, this time at the national championship celebration at the Smith Center. (Photo by J. D. Lyon Jr.)

Thousands of fans watched the bus cruise Franklin on the Smith Center video boards, then roared when the team brought the trophy to the arena. The players and coaches had been gone for a full week. When the players returned to their dorm rooms, they found notes from fellow students.

"You made our senior year," the notes read. "Thank you for giving us unforgettable memories. You are legends."

Over the next few days and weeks, Carolina players would be stopped in airports and at restaurants by Tar Heel fans who just wanted to thank them

for winning a title. At the Wells Fargo Championship in Wilmington in May, fans dashed across the golf course just to shake Luke Maye's hand. A couple of weeks earlier, he'd thrown out the first pitch at a Carolina baseball game and watched as fans lined up for his signature . . . while they completely ignored tennis all-time greats Steffi Graf and Andre Agassi, who were seated on the row in front of him. Pinson and Meeks each had their jerseys retired at their respective high schools. Hicks, Britt, and Meeks graduated on Mother's Day, as did Stilman White and Kanler Coker, combining their title with an important academic achievement.

"Where I came from, nobody went to a major college or won a national championship," Hicks said. "I am so blessed to have this opportunity. Coach gave me a chance to be part of this team, and I am so thankful for that. This was such a great way to end my career here."

The best post-championship compliment of all might have come from a familiar source. In the hours and days after the championship, Marcus Paige, just finishing his first professional season, considered the events of the past 12 months. He had perhaps the most fun he'd ever had playing basketball. He had suffered the most heartbreaking defeat in his sports career. And he had watched his friends and teammates get back to the exact same spot and, this time, find a way to win.

Paige composed a text message to the 2017 Tar Heels.

"Do you guys realize you really did it?" he wrote. "You went back and finished the job. Don't forget that. Against all odds, you went back and won it. Be proud of yourselves. You will forever be legends. You are going down in history."

National Championship Team & Player Highlights

- Carolina won its sixth NCAA championship with a 71–65 win over Gonzaga in Glendale, Ariz.

- The Tar Heels went 33–7, including 14–4 in the ACC, 1–1 in the ACC Tournament, and 6–0 in the NCAA Tournament.

- Carolina won the ACC regular-season title by two games over Florida State, Notre Dame, and Louisville.

- Carolina was the No. 1 seed and champion of the South Regional.

- Carolina is one of three schools to win the NCAA title one year after losing in the national championship game and the only school to accomplish that twice (UNC in 1982 and 2017, Duke in 1991, and Kentucky in 1998).

- Point guard Joel Berry II was the Final Four's Most Outstanding Player. Berry scored a game-high 22 points and had six assists, two steals, and a blocked shot in the national championship game versus Gonzaga.

- Berry became the first player since Hall-of-Famer Bill Walton in 1972–73 to score 20 or more points in consecutive national championship games (20 in 2016 versus Villanova).

- Berry and James Worthy are the only Tar Heels to win ACC Tournament MVP and Final Four MVP honors. Worthy won both in 1982; Berry won the ACC Tournament MVP in 2016.

- Forwards Kennedy Meeks and Justin Jackson joined Berry on the All–Final Four team.

- Carolina held four of its six NCAA Tournament opponents to under 75 points. This was the first season that UNC played six NCAA Tournament games and held the opponents to under 44 percent shooting from the floor in every game.

- Jackson led UNC in scoring in the 2017 NCAA Tournament with 117 points (19.5 per game). That's the third-most points and third-highest average in a six-game NCAA Tournament series by a Tar Heel.

- Jackson also led UNC in the NCAA Tournament with 22 assists, 15 three-pointers, and 9 steals.

- Meeks averaged 12.2 points and grabbed 69 rebounds (11.5 per game) in the 2017 NCAA Tournament. The 69 rebounds are the most in any single six-game NCAA Tournament run by a Tar Heel, and he is the fourth to average a double-double in points and rebounds in an NCAA Tournament, joining Pete Brennan (1957), Antawn Jamison (1998), and Sean May (2005).

- Meeks led UNC in field-goal percentage (.643), blocked shots (13), and steals (nine) in the NCAA Tournament.

- Jackson is second in UNC history with 239 points in NCAA Tournament play; Meeks is second in rebounds with 139.

- Luke Maye was the South Regional MVP after scoring a career-high 16 points with 12 rebounds in the Sweet 16 win over Butler and a career-high 17 points and the game-winning shot with 0.3 seconds to play in the win over Kentucky in the regional final.

Hugs and tears flowed freely after Carolina's 71–65 win over Gonzaga. (Photo by J. D. Lyon Jr.)

Justin Jackson's championship-clinching dunk helped him move to No. 2 all-time in scoring in UNC's NCAA Tournament history. (Photo by Jeffrey A. Camarati)

Graduating seniors Coker, Hicks, Meeks, White, and Britt with Coach Williams. (Photo by Jeffrey A. Camarati)

- Maye became the first nonstarter in the NCAA Tournament to win regional MVP honors since Massachusetts' Marcus Camby in 1996.

- Berry and Jackson joined Maye on the All–South Regional team.

- Carolina won four NCAA Tournament games by seven points or less, the first team to do that since Arizona in 1997.

- Carolina's 75–73 win over Kentucky in the regional final and its 77–76 win over Oregon in the national semifinal marked the first time UNC won consecutive NCAA games by two points or less since 1969, when it defeated Duquesne, 79–78, in the East semifinal and Davidson, 87–85, in the East final.

- The win over Gonzaga was the 14th NCAA Tournament win for Nate Britt, Isaiah Hicks, and Meeks, which equaled the second-most in Carolina history.

- Carolina played in its 20th Final Four, the most in college basketball history. The Tar Heels have won 123 NCAA Tournament games, second all-time.

- Carolina allowed 141 points in the Final Four, the same number of points UNC allowed in the 2005 and 2009 Final Fours.

- Jackson became the 14th Tar Heel to win ACC Player-of-the-Year honors and the 18th to earn consensus first-team All-America honors.

- Jackson (first team) and Berry (second team) earned All-ACC honors.

- Jackson set the UNC single-season record with 105 three-pointers and scored 731 points, the fifth-most in a season by a Tar Heel.

- Carolina led the nation in rebounding (43.7 per game), rebound margin (+12.3), and offensive rebounds (15.8 per game).

- Britt and Hicks set a UNC record by playing in 59 ACC wins (regular season and tournament), and they played in 151 games, second-most in UNC and ACC history.

(Photo by J. D. Lyon Jr.)

Hubert Davis

You see all different types of emotions in this photo. There is happiness that we won. There's sadness from having lost the Villanova game the year before. There's the pain of some of the things we've been through off the court. There's happiness for Coach Williams, and for Coach Smith and Coach Guthridge. There's redemption that I felt personally from the 1991 Final Four. There's tears from losing the NBA championship in Game Seven in 1994. All of those things are coming together in this moment.

The Gonzaga game was more than just a game. It was more than Carolina and Gonzaga. I can't put into words the pain of what has gone on with this university and how it has impacted this program. You combine that with the feeling of losing in the championship game in 2016, with the way we lost, and it was beyond devastating. Then we were able to come back and do it in 2017. To me, I can't even separate those two years. It was a two-year journey, and we finished it with a national championship.

Roy Williams Career Highlights

- Inducted into the Naismith Basketball Hall of Fame in 2007.

- Won NCAA championships at UNC in 2005, 2009, and 2017 and led Kansas and Carolina to runner-up finishes in 1991, 2003, and 2016.

- Sixth coach to win three or more NCAA titles, with John Wooden (10), Mike Krzyzewski (5), Jim Calhoun (3), Bob Knight (3), and Adolph Rupp (3).

- First coach to win three NCAA titles at his alma mater.

- Third coach to take teams to six national championship games, with John Wooden (10) and Mike Krzyzewski (9).

- Led his team to the Final Four for the ninth time in his head-coaching career (five at Carolina, four at Kansas).

- Second all-time in NCAA Tournament victories with 76 and in games with 100.

- Fourth all-time in Final Fours with nine (four at Kansas and five at UNC) behind only John Wooden, Mike Krzyzewski, and Dean Smith.

- Led Carolina and Kansas to 12 No. 1 NCAA Tournament seeds, second-most all-time.

- Won 11 more NCAA Tournament games (51) in the last 16 years than any coach in the country.

- Led UNC to 42 NCAA Tournament wins in the last 14 years, nine more than any other school.

- Reached the Elite Eight 13 times, including eight times in 14 years at Carolina.

- Reached the Sweet Sixteen 18 times in 27 NCAA Tournament appearances, nine at Carolina and nine at Kansas.

- Won all 27 NCAA Tournament first-round games, the best record in opening round play in NCAA Tournament history.

- Earned a No. 1 seed in the NCAA Tournament 12 times (second all-time), including seven times in 14 seasons at Carolina.

- Led Carolina to the 2017 ACC regular-season championship, the eighth title in the last 13 years. No other ACC school or coach has won more than three ACC regular-season titles in Williams' 14 years as Carolina's head coach.

- Led North Carolina and Kansas to 17 first-place finishes in conference play in 29 seasons.

- Eighth all-time with 816 wins as Division I head coach.

- Sixth all-time in 20-win seasons with 27 behind Mike Krzyzewski (33), Jim Boeheim (32), Dean Smith (30), Bob Knight (29) and Lute Olson (28).

- Won 30 games a dozen times (seven seasons at Carolina), and is second all-time in 30-win seasons in NCAA history (14 by Krzyzewski).

- Ninth Division I coach to win 800 games (#800 was against Syracuse on January 16, 2017).

- Won 800 games in fewer seasons (29) than any coach in history; the previous fastest were Dean Smith and Mike Krzyzewski (33 seasons).

- Second-fastest to 800 wins in games (1,012), behind Rupp (972 games).

- Won 387 of his first 500 games at UNC, more wins than any coach in ACC history in his first 500 games.

- Averaged 28.1 wins per season, first all-time among coaches with 800 or more wins.

Carolina advanced to the Final Four for an unprecedented 20th time.

(Photo by J. D. Lyon Jr.)

- Second in 30-win seasons with 12, including seven at UNC.

- Led UNC to a No. 5 finish in the final Associated Press poll and a No.1 finish in the USA Today/Coaches Poll. It was his 18th top-10 finish and 14th top-five finish in the AP poll.

- Led UNC to a 5–4 road record in ACC play, the 11th time in 14 seasons the Tar Heels posted a winning record on the road in the ACC.

- Tied for third all-time with 75 ACC road wins, behind only Krzyzewski (171) and Smith (133).

- Second all-time in winning percentage in ACC road games at 64.1 percent (75–42).

- Won more games (17) than any coach in Maui Invitational history and is the second coach to win at least four Maui titles. Has won the Maui Invitational at Carolina in 2004–05, 2008–09, and 2016–17 and at Kansas in 1996–97.

- Sixth all-time and first in winning percentage (.791) among active coaches with at least 20 years of experience.

- Fourth in wins by an ACC head coach in all games (398) and in ACC games (181).

- Led Carolina to 10 AP top-10 finishes in 14 years (18 top 10's in 29 years as a head coach).

- Coached two Academic All-Americas of the Year (Jacque Vaughn and Tyler Zeller), seven Academic All-Americas (tied fourth), and the ACC Scholar-Athlete of the Year in four of last seven years.

- Coached three Bob Cousy Award winners (nation's top point guard), four National Players of the Year, and 17 first-team All-Americas (most recent is Justin Jackson in 2017).

North Carolina governor Roy Cooper hosted the Tar Heels at the governor's mansion in Raleigh. (Photo by Matt Bowers)

Roy Williams is second in NCAA Tournament history with 76 wins in 100 games. (Photo by Kevin Cox/Getty Images)

Acknowledgments

The chance to chronicle North Carolina's sixth NCAA championship was an incredible opportunity. We were lucky enough to be there from fall conditioning in September through the basketball banquet in April, but it would not have been possible to tell the full story of the 2017 national championship without extensive help from dozens of people.

The first, of course, are the Tar Heel players and coaches. It's one thing to win a national championship; it's quite another to have to sit down and relive it for hours at a time after the season. We are very grateful to Nate Britt, Kanler Coker, Isaiah Hicks, Kennedy Meeks, Stilman White, Joel Berry, Justin Jackson, Theo Pinson, Aaron Rohlman, Luke Maye, Kenny Williams, Tony Bradley, Brandon Robinson, Shea Rush, and Seventh Woods for both their achievements on the court and their constant willingness to provide insight off the court. Marcus Paige helped put 2017 in context as part of a two-year process. The Tar Heel managers—Chase Bengel, Emily Brickner, John Bumgarner, Tyler Hagan, Forrest Reynolds, and Maria Vanderford—might do more work for less recognition than anyone in the program. The office staff of Kaye Chase, Cynthia Friend, and Nadia Lynch kept everything organized.

As Roy Williams often says, the team was led by a Carolina coaching staff that is the best in the country. Assistant coaches Hubert Davis, C. B. McGrath, and Steve Robinson and director of operations Brad Frederick were happy to explain a key decision or a point of the scouting report. Eric Hoots and Sean May were equally helpful and always willing to assist. Doug Halverson and Jonas Sahratian probably had a bigger role in this season than they wished and helped us understand the importance of that role. Shane Parrish was the equipment gatekeeper, which means he has to tell people "no" more often than he might like. Clint Gwaltney laid the groundwork for the season and was the keeper of the toolbox.

Coach Williams gave us four hours for an interview one night in April and then concluded the marathon session with, "Now, just let me know what else you need." He is a Hall of Famer in every aspect.

We wanted this book to be a little different, and John Lyon's photos were the asset that allowed us to give you a true behind-the-scenes look at a national title team. This is a championship book unlike any we've done, and John's dedication to his work and chemistry with the players—and the photos produced by that chemistry—are the reasons why. We are also appreciative of the other photographers represented in this book, especially Jeffrey Camarati, who ably managed the tens of thousands of pictures that were considered for publication.

Once we decided to tell the complete story of the 2016–17 season, we knew we would need assistance from those who frequently see behind the curtain. The input of Rusty Carter, Joe Holladay, Hunter Morin, Cody Plott, Bill Puckett, Scott Williams, and Wanda Williams was invaluable to painting the full picture of this unforgettable season.

With the thousands of air miles this year came dozens of dinners, late-night flights, and early morning breakfasts. Thanks to Ben Alexander, Jones Angell, Ray Gaskins, Jon Leggette, Eric Montross, Billy Puryear, Josh Reavis, and Jenn Townsend for being part of those, and to Eric Church for providing the soundtrack on so many of those late nights.

So many helped us produce this book. Rachel Brittain, Ani Garrigo, Kendall Harden, Matt Hodgin, Olivia Ingram, Conor Lynch, Kim Rivers, Liz Robins, and Matti Smith—student assistants in the athletic communications office—helped transcribe hours of interviews with the players and sorted through hundreds of photos. Brian Stehlin at Getty Images and Annie Pratt at USA Today Sports Images provided assistance obtaining photos. And Mark Simpson-Vos, Jay Mazzocchi, and Kim Bryant at UNC Press gave us a wonderful book for people to enjoy.

There are two other key groups without whom this book would be impossible and pointless. Our families are willing to put life as we know it on hold during the Carolina Basketball season. Steve has been fortunate to be part of 11 Final Fours and four national titles at Carolina, but this was the first time his wife, Jeanne, and his kids, Ryan and Emilie, were in the stands to see the Tar Heels win and cut down the championship nets. For that reason, the opportunity to share some of the behind-the-scenes moments that he sees every day made working on this book such a labor of love. Crystal, Sam, and Chloe Bowers tolerate the job that takes Matt away from them so often. National championship runs are great fun, but coming home afterward is always better.

I truly believe Jennifer Lucas can do anything in the world; I marvel daily that she chose to share her life with me. Our kids—Virginia, Drew, McKay, and Asher—gave me one of the most unforgettable days ever when we rode UTVs in the morning and watched a national championship in the evening.

And finally, thank you to Carolina fans, the people who wait up late at night to read the newest GoHeels.com column or arrive an hour early to pack an arena just to take photos of the Tar Heels in the layup line. Carolina Basketball fans don't get enough credit. You are the best in the country, and your passion makes this the best job in the world.